AF407428

LOVE SOMEONE WITH ANXIETY

Understand and Help a Partner suffering from an Anxiety Disorder

Birgit Roswell

© COPYRIGHT 2020 BY BIRGIT ROSWELL - ALL RIGHTS RESERVED.

This book is geared towards providing exact and reliable information in regard to the topic and issue covered. The publication is sold with the idea that the publisher is not required to render accounting, officially permitted, or otherwise, qualified services. If advice is necessary, legal or professional, a practiced individual in the profession should be ordered.

In no way is it legal to reproduce, duplicate, or transmit any part of this document in either electronic means or in printed format. Recording of this publication is strictly prohibited, and any storage of this document is not allowed unless with written permission from the publisher.

All rights reserved.

The information provided herein is stated to be truthful and consistent, in that any liability, in terms of inattention or otherwise, by any usage or abuse of any policies, processes, or directions contained within is the solitary and utter responsibility of the recipient reader. Under no circumstances will any legal responsibility or blame be held against the publisher for any reparation, damages, or monetary loss due to the information herein, either directly or indirectly.

Respective authors own all copyrights not held by the publisher. The information herein is offered for informational purposes solely and is universal as so. The presentation of the information is without a contract or any type of guarantee assurance.

The trademarks that are used are without any consent, and the publication of the trademark is without permission or backing by the trademark owner. All trademarks and brands within this book are for clarifying purposes only and are owned by the owners themselves, not affiliated with this document.

Dedication

This book is dedicated to all those whose loved ones are currently living with unimaginable anxiety disorders and to all those that have spent their time, and skills loving their beloved without measure despite dealing with this unfortunate condition.

Table of Content

INTRODUCTION 1

CHAPTER ONE 6

Understanding the Role and Impact of Anxiety 6

Major Types of Anxiety Disorder 9

Effects of Anxiety on Physical and Mental

Health 15

Classical Difference between Stress and Anxiety

.... 18

The Impact of Anxiety Disorders on the Victim

.... 20

Causes of Anxiety Disorder 21

Diagnosis 31

What to Do When Your Partner Becomes

Anxious? 32

Treatment 33

Counseling 35

A Combination of Medications 36

Prevention 38

Symptoms of Anxiety.....................................39

Identifying Anxiety Triggers 40

CHAPTER TWO...45

How Anxiety Affects Relationships- The Bad and Ugly...45

Required Steps to Managing Relationship Anxiety...48

What Anxiety Is Doing to Your Partner 51

How Anxiety Can Influence Your Relationship .53

Dating Someone with Anxiety 57

How to Cope with the Situation......................57

Managing Your Reactions to the Anxiety.........60

Tested and Proven Ways to Support Your Partner 63

Challenges of Living with Anxious Partner 77

CHAPTER THREE.................................80

How to Improve Communication with an Anxious Partner..................................... 80

What You Should Not Do 88

Nutritional Foods That Relief Anxiety 89

How to Respond and Deal with My Partner's Specific Type of Anxiety 97

CHAPTER FOUR 101

Anger Management: How to overcome it and Get the life of your partner back 101

Understanding the Concept of Anger 105

How Will Anger Create Problems to You? 108

What Is Anger Management?........................ 110

Signs That Your Loved One Need Anger Management Help.. 112

How to Get Out of Anger............................... 112

The Root Cause of Anger 119

Constructive Ways of Handling Angry Feelings

....121

Overcoming Explosive Anger 122

CHAPTER FIVE 138

Self-Care Tips When You Love Someone with

Anxiety...138

What to Do When Anxiety Takes Over Your

Partner's Concentration.................................147

How Meditation Can Actually Transform the

Brain 152

Fascinating Things Anxiety Does to the Brain 159

What Happens in The Brain When Someone Is

Stressed Or Anxious? 164

How Your Anxious Partner Can Boost Their

Concentration at Work 165

High-Functioning Social Anxiety.....................173

Transiting from Acute Social Anxiety to High-Functioning.. 180

Things You Shouldn't Say to an Anxious Partner

.... 185

Surprising Health Benefits of Hugging 192

EVALUATION AND CONCLUSION 198

How to Deal with Anxiety in a Relationship .. 213

CONCLUSION... 224

Introduction

It is really a difficult task to love someone with anxiety. Over the years, many people have tried effortlessly to do this to no avail. Living with anxious partner can lead to a sense of hopelessness, anger and resentment on your side. The essence of this book is to help you and your anxious loved one to build a stronger personal connection, better communication, live together happily, and avoid negative behaviors.

This book doesn't blame anyone, instead it offers practical step on how to understand anxious behaviors and how to respond to it promptly and efficiently. If your loved one is suffering from anxiety, then this book is for you. You will learn how to improve your relationships with effective communication strategies.

For decades now, I have met countless partners who are living with someone with anxiety. Hundreds of them have reached out to me seeking for professional help. Many have gotten relieved; many are still undergoing the process.

It can be horribly stressful to date or marry someone with anxiety issues. Sometimes you may be tempted to think that anxiety is the third person in the relationship, an unfortunate person that wriggles between you and your partner, an unwelcome guest, sowing doubts and confusion here and there.

This is not what you bargained for; no one prepared you for this. You didn't receive any education on dating, more or less dating someone with a striking mental illness. Regardless of all these facts, anxiety is bad and doesn't have to come in between your relationship. There should be a way out. This book is the way out.

Anxiety doesn't have to dictate the status of your relationship or, put a stain or break your relationship. Understanding the nature of anxiety in general and how it affects your relationship with your partner will help you to appreciate, cherish and love each other more deeply. Educating yourself on this fact will offer you some relief.

This book breaks down all the essential details you need to know and do when you love someone with anxiety issues; how to support yourself and your beloved, understand how anxiety can influence your relationship, learn how to cope with your mental health and lots more.

Remain focus, and keep working hard, so that anxiety doesn't succeed in becoming the third person in your relationship.

Anxiety disorder can affect a person's life emotionally, psychologically, physically, and mentally. It can make the person's life to be dramatically impaired.

Although, outwardly there may not be noticeable signs of mental illness, but anxiety disorder can cause untold lifestyle impairment and this can leave the patient to be confused, frightened, and frustrated. Patients of anxiety disorder are generally determined, compassionate, creative and intelligent.

Though, some may become discouraged, frightened, confused, and seemingly hypochondriac when anxiety disorder develops. Some of the battles they fight internally are often all-consuming, a battle that it is only someone that had gone through the crucibles of anxiety disorder and eventual total healing can understand. Their struggle is real. This mental condition can affect a person in multiple ways. It is better experienced than imagined or described.

Fortunately, and happily too, anxiety disorder can be overcome. However, this process requires active work, energy and more time than most people think. During the recovery process, your partner needs all the help you can give, and this book offers some tested and proven ways you can help them overcome their struggle with anxiety disorder.

Finally, this is that book they need to read, a veritable and highly resourceful goldmine. Among other things, it provides robust answers on how to live in the present moment, resolve anxiety issues and promote inner peace for both partners.

Take up and read!

CHAPTER ONE

Understanding the Role and Impact of Anxiety

Anxiety is one of the most prevalent mental health problems around the world. This is one of the contending issues that are still under-diagnosed, under-treated and under-reported. In most people, anxiety triggers disproportionate and inappropriate responses to perceived threats, thereby leading to intrusive and persistent symptoms linked with anxiety disorders such as obsessive behaviors, phobias and panic. All these have a devastating effect on our lives.

Anxious partners respond or identify dangers in 'flight or fight' mode. Anxiety can make the sufferer to deal with difficult challenges. Persistent anxiety causes real emotional damage.

Anxiety is capable of having a debilitating and truly distressing impact on both our physical and mental health. In recent times, there have been arguments and counter-arguments on this issue. Some analysts maintain that we are living in the 'age of anxiety'. A recent survey by the Mental Health Foundation confirms that one in every five people feel anxious 'a lot of the time or nearly all of the time'. This is really a disturbing trend, considering the fact that more people are anxious today than they were 10 years ago.

Experiencing too much of anxiety today means the patient risk becoming overwhelmed or unable to balance their lives, relax and recover. Finding an inner peace becomes an important role to our wellbeing.

Anxiety is an essential part of humanity or natural human emotional impulse to circumstances surrounding our lives. It is our duty to recognize when people around us especially our beloved spouse is experiencing distressing levels of anxiety due to unforeseen life events or circumstances.

At some point in life, people experience or express feelings of anxiety whether they are preparing for a job interview, expecting a new baby, or even meeting a partner's immediate family for the first time, learning to sing, learning to read or write for the first time, preparing for an examination, learning to drive, learning to speak in public and lots more.

Anxiety is closely associated with alterations to our mental wellbeing; it can come as apprehension, worry, physical symptoms such as adrenaline and raised heart rate. It is most likely going to affect our physical reaction temporarily until we have learnt how to cope with it or the source of the anxiety has passed.

Anxiety alerts us to potentially harmful things that we may likely worry about. It enables us to evaluate these threats and respond to them in the right way, perhaps by remaining focused to our attention, or quickening our reflexes.

It is a behavioral, physiological and psychological state we share with other lower animals when we are confronted with a potential threat to our survival instinct or overall wellbeing.

Anxiety triggers specific behavioral patterns like a chronic sense of dread, tension or worry in anticipation of some imaginary, unclear or ill-defined misfortune. It increases our body's expectancy, arousal, neurobiological activity, and connotes lingering apprehension to stressful situations.

For most anxious people, their levels of anxiety get worse over time. This can impair their ability to function effectively at home, work, or social functions. It can also interfere drastically with their relationship with their partners, family and friends.

Major Types of Anxiety Disorder

Anxiety disorder is a common phenomenon in both adult and children. The National Institute of Mental Health says that about 4% of U.S adults and nearly 6% of teens have severe anxiety disorders. Below are major types of anxiety disorders:

Generalized Anxiety Disorder (GAD)

This is a chronic disorder characterized by persistent anxious feelings or worries for no logical reason. Victims of this disorder worry a lot about several concerns such as their levels of finances or health problems.

They always have a feeling that something bad may likely happen to their lives. Symptoms of generalized anxiety disorder include difficulty concentrating, muscle tension, irritability, restlessness, generally feeling on edge and sleep problems. Some victims of generalized anxiety disorders are unable to identify the root cause of their anxiety.

Panic Disorder

This is characterized by recurrent panic attacks or spontaneous feelings of anxiety. Symptoms of panic disorder include feelings of dread, rapid heart rate, chest pain, a pounding heart or heart palpitations, a feeling of choking or shortness of breath, sudden or brief attacks, nausea, and dizziness, breathing difficulties, trembling and sweating.

Panic attacks happens accidentally oftentimes without potential warning. Panic disorder can also trigger other forms of anxiety. Victims of panic disorder become fearful about life and living, this can restrict their levels of happiness, taste of life and normal activities. Panic attacks tend to escalate rapidly and might last for a few minutes or hours or even days.

Panic attacks usually occur in some people after a prolonged stress or frightening experience. Some uninformed people experiencing panic attack may think it is a life-threatening illness.

Phobias

Phobias are characterized by developing intense fears about distressing or intrusive certain objects such as snakes, spiders and situations such as flying in airplanes, boat cruising, fear of heights (acrophobia), fear of tight spaces (claustrophobia), and lots more.

The victim may have unimaginable urge to avoid the feared situation or object.

Social Anxiety Disorder

This is also called social phobia. Victims of this disorder are nervous about certain situations where they might feel judged or embarrassed. Typically, they fear spending quality time in social settings, feel less human in front of others, worry about offending or being rejected by others. This paralyzing fear of social situations can leave the victim to be alone or feel ashamed and become emotionally withdrawn.

Symptoms include difficulty in making friends, feeling shaky or worrying endlessly for days before a social event, becoming nauseous or sweaty when relating with people in a social setting, avoiding social functions etc.

According to the Anxiety and Depression Association of America, about 15 million American adults are currently living with social anxiety disorder. About one-third of these people wait for a decade before seeking for help.

Obsessive-Compulsive Disorder

This is all about having uncontrollable thoughts, persistent feelings, rituals or routines (compulsions). Commonest examples include relentlessly checking work for errors or repeated counting, compulsive habitual hand washing due to fear of contacting germs, aggressive impulses, concerns about cleanliness and much more.

Post-Traumatic Stress Disorder (PTSD)

This can be triggered after a prolonged emotional or physical traumatic experience such as crime, fatal accident or natural disaster. Symptoms include frightening thoughts, war, physical attack, natural disasters, nightmares, and flashbacks of the trauma. These things oftentimes interfere with the person's daily activity for months or years after the traumatic experience. This type of disorder may be triggered without warning.

Agoraphobia

Agoraphobia is characterized by a fear and avoidance of situations, events and places, from where it might be extremely difficult to escape should something happen or if the person becomes trapped.

Some analysts regard this as a phobia of the outdoors and open spaces. A victim of agoraphobia may have a fear of using public transport, elevators, leaving home or even visiting malls.

Selective Mutism (Social Phobia)

This is the type of phobia that most people experience in which they are unable to speak in certain places, situations or contexts such as social events, school, workplace even though they may have avid verbal communication skills and competencies around familiar people and friends.

This is also referred as social phobia. Selective Mutism includes a wide range of feelings including a fear of intimacy, anxiety around rejection or humiliation and stage fright. This disorder can motivate the victim to avoid unfamiliar human contact and public situations to the point that they find it extremely difficult to live daily.

Effects of Anxiety on Physical and Mental Health

People from time to time experience anxiety, but chronic anxiety can have a negative impact on the quality of life, physical health and behavioral changes. For example, your partner may experience anxiety preparing for a job interview, while discussing with employer or addressing a group.

Anxiety increases your heart and breathing rate, and blood flow to your brain. The effect is that it can prepare you when you are confronted with an intense situation. If the situation becomes too intense, you might start to feel nauseous or lightheaded. Obviously, this can have a negative effect on the victim's mental and physical health.

Anxiety disorder can be triggered at any age, but it is usually rampant at middle age. The National Institute of Mental Health says that women are more liable to suffer anxiety disorder than men. Substance use disorder or serious medical condition can lead to anxiety disorder. Let's take a cursory look at its effect in our lives:

Central Nervous System

Panic disorders and long-term anxiety can increase the frequency of symptoms including depression, dizziness, and headaches. When someone is anxious, the brain will flood the nervous system with chemicals and hormones that will help the victim to respond to a threat. Two commonest examples are cortisol and adrenaline. Long-term exposure to cortisol can lead to excessive weight gain, and this will be harmful to your health in the long run.

Cardiovascular System

Anxiety disorders can lead to chest pain, heart palpitations and rapid heart rate. The victim may be at an increased risk of heart disease and high blood pressure. Heart disease patients may develop coronary events.

Excretory and Digestive Systems

Anxiety disorders affect the victim's digestive and excretory systems negatively. The victim may experience loss of appetite, diarrhea, nausea, stomach aches, irritable bowel syndrome, constipation, vomiting and many more.

Immune System

Anxiety disorders can increase your breathing rate and impulse, thereby making your brain to get more oxygen. Thus, this will prepare the victim to respond accurately and swiftly to an impending intense situation. The immune system will get an instant brief boost. As soon as the stress passes, the body will return to its normal performing rate.

However, if this anxiety persists for a long time, your body may never return to its normal functioning capacity, thereby rendering regular vaccines futile and impotent. This will weaken the immune system, thereby making the victim vulnerable to frequent illnesses and viral infections.

Respiratory System

Anxiety disorders cause shallow breathing, obstructive pulmonary disease, trigger asthma symptoms.

Classical Difference between Stress and Anxiety

At different times, people use the terms 'stress' and 'anxiety' interchangeably. But, both are actually different sensations. When your loved one feel stressed, it is because of a known cause- may be they are having issues dealing with kids or working on a tight deadline. This stress can manifest in various feelings of irritability, sadness, or anger as well. Chronic stress has been linked with heart disease, weight gain and weakened immune system, among other issues.

While anxiety is a specific dread or feeling of fear. It may or may not have a known trigger. Sometimes people living with anxiety disorder will wake up feeling anxious for no known reason. Anxiety can also be triggered by a chronic stress. Someone who experiences constant surge of stress hormones is at a higher risk of developing generalized anxiety.

The wear and tear caused by the brain due to anxiety or chronic stress could be as a result of dementia or depression. Some experts believe that some of the damages incurred by chronic stress and anxiety can be reversed.

For decades, it was erroneously believed that when a brain lost volume, it will be gone forever. But recent scientific discoveries have proved otherwise. The human brain is plastic; this means that they are capable of going through transformational change. The brain undergoes some degrees of regeneration and re-growth overtime.

The antidote is to always protect the brain from any damages incurred from the effects of anxiety and chronic stress. It is always good to find great ways of managing them so that they won't affect you or your loved one's health. Luckily, studies have made available some medical and non-medical therapies for these conditions.

The Impact of Anxiety Disorders on the Victim

The danger of anxiety disorder is that it can affect both the sufferer and the partner. When infected, it will undermine the victim's capacity to function properly in their daily roles such as common social interactions, parenting, and working effectively.

Obviously, this will affect the person's interpersonal relationship to the extent that spouse, family members, friends and workplace colleagues will be affected. This disorder obstructs how a person react, and processes emotions, thereby making the victim to appear unsettling and vague.

Causes of Anxiety Disorder

The causes of anxiety disorders are quite complex. Sometimes, anxiety disorder may develop without an external trigger. Also, a combination of one or more causes below can trigger it such as difficult physical health, experiences and personality factors.

Anxiety disorder is a mental condition that can cause tension, fear or worry, extreme physical symptoms like panic attacks and chest pain. Anxiety disorders can be triggered by a combination of factors such as environmental conditions and genetics. Also, some experiences, emotions and events could trigger it or even make it worse.

These factors are called triggers. What triggers anxiety in one person may be different from what triggers it in another person. Some people observe that they have multiple triggers. Thus, identifying the trigger is the first step towards managing the situation.

Here are some complicated networks of causes:

Family History of Mental Health Issues

Anxiety disorders are genetically related; some people whose parents have anxiety disorders are more likely to be potential victims someday.

However, having a parent, sibling or relative who experience anxiety is not a necessary condition that you may automatically develop anxiety complications.

Personality Factors

Studies have proven that people with certain elements of personality traits are more liable to develop anxiety issues. For example, people who are easily frustrated, perfectionists, inhibited, want to control everything or lack self-esteem.

Consistent Stressful Events

People can develop anxiety due to one or more stressful situations. Some common triggers include job change or work stress, change in living conditions, giving birth or pregnancy, relationship or family concerns, emotional shock arising from a traumatic incidence, emotional, physical, sexual or verbal abuse, loss of a loved one.

Physical Health Issues

Chronic physical condition can trigger anxiety. Some of the common anxiety related conditions include heart disease, hypertension, asthma, diabetes, overactive thyroid etc. When any of these happens, the patient is advised to see a doctor for adequate prescription.

Anxiety can be triggered by an upsetting or difficult health diagnosis like chronic illness or cancer. This could trigger or even complicate the situation. This type of trigger is extremely noticeable because of the personal and immediate result it produces.

Health-related anxiety can be reduced by talking with a therapist, visiting your doctor or being proactive about the situation. All these can help to manage your emotions.

Substance Abuse

Many people try to manage anxiety issues by using alcohol or other drugs. This is not a helpful strategy, because it may lead to developing other health complications together with anxiety condition.

Excessive use of alcohol or other drugs may calm the situation for awhile, but overtly aggravate the anxiety conditions. Getting checked and assistance from a mental health professional will bring a perpetual solution to the issue.

Environmental Factors

Some factors in the environment can contribute greatly to anxiety such as stress from a partner or relationship problems, difficulties at workplace, home, school, financial predicament, low oxygen levels and many more.

Genetic factors

Anxiety disorders are genetically related; some people whose parents have anxiety disorders are more likely to be potential victims someday.

Medical factors

Some acute medical conditions are vulnerable to anxiety disorder such as symptoms of a disease, significant lifestyle adjustments, stress from an excruciating surgery or prolonged recovery or the effects of a medication, restricted movements, and pain.

Brain Chemistry

Genetic factors or traumatic experiences can alter brain function that wouldn't have caused anxiety in the first place. Neurologists and psychologists define anxiety disorders as disruptions to electrical and hormonal signals in the brain.

Use or Withdrawal from Illicit Substance

The effect of using or withdrawing from an illicit substance can be a key trigger to anxiety disorder. For example, your partner may respond to stress at work or mid life crisis by taking illicit substances or drinking more alcohol. This can lead to further complications and increasing anxiety levels or other possible causes.

Medications

Some medications can trigger anxiety such as weight loss medications, cough and congestion medications, and birth control pills. Talk with your doctor if you observe any reaction in your body after taking these medications.

Caffeine

Caffeine can worsen or trigger anxiety. Most patients of social anxiety disorder and panic disorder are extremely sensitive to devastating effects of caffeine. Taking non-caffeinated options remains the real deal.

Skipping Meals

Whenever someone is hungry, their blood sugar will drop. This could lead to rumbling tummy and jittery hands and may in adversely trigger anxiety. Eating a balanced diet is healthy for many reasons. It supplies enough nutrients and energy to your body.

If it is not convenient for you to eat three meals per day, you can substitute it with health snacks. Remember, being hungry can affect your mood drastically. Eating a healthy diet will help to prevent anxiety, agitation or feelings of nervousness and low blood sugar.

Negative Thinking

Just like the mind controls your body, the same way anxiety affects your actions. When you are upset, angry or frustrated, the words you speak to yourself could trigger feelings of anxiety.

When you are in this situation, it is advisable you re-focus your feelings and language, so that you won't use a lot of negative thoughts on yourself. Working with a therapist could be very helpful.

Financial Concerns

Excessive worries about having debt, money fears, unexpected bills or saving money can trigger anxiety. Managing this type of anxiety may require a professional assistance from a qualified financial advisor. Feeling or knowing that there is a helpful partner or companion around you may ease the tension.

Social Events or Parties

Certain events or parties that require you to interact or speak with unfamiliar people or total strangers can trigger feelings of anxiety. To help your partner ease this worry, you can go along with them when possible. But, it is also suitable to work with a professional who will help to find coping mechanisms that will help your partner manage these events in the long term.

Conflict

Conflict is a major trigger of anxiety such as arguments, counterarguments and relationship issues. All these could either trigger or worsen the situation. If conflict triggers your partner, then you may suggest they learn conflict resolution strategies. You can teach them the little you know about it or by sending them on a few hours training on conflict resolution and people relations. Alternatively, you can talk with a mental health counselor or a therapist to learn how to manage these conflicts.

Stress

Consistent stressors like missing your flight or train or traffic jam can trigger anxiety. Chronic or long-term stress and health problems can trigger or even worsen the symptoms. Stress can also make your partner to skip their meals, not getting enough sleep, and drinking alcohol.

Preventing or treating stress requires learning relevant coping strategies. Talking with a counselor or therapist can help you to recognize the cause of the stress as well as handle them when they become problematic or overwhelming.

Speaking in Public or Performances

Speaking in public or speaking to a boss, making a presentation, reading aloud in a board meeting or even performing in a competition could trigger anxiety.

If your partner's job requires any of these, you can recommend a therapist or doctor to your partner who will inspire them and equip them on how to be comfortable in these settings.

More so, positive reinforcements from colleagues, peers, friends and family can help them to feel more confident, focused and comfortable.

Personal Triggers

Some personal triggers may be extremely difficult to identify. However, connecting your partner with a mental health specialist can help to resolve this issue. Some common examples of personal triggers include a traumatic event, a bad memory in your life. People with post-traumatic stress disorder (PTSD) often experience this issue from environmental triggers.

It takes time and energy to identify personal triggers. But, it is noble to do so, because it will help your partner to overcome them.

Diagnosis

Anxiety disorders can be diagnosed by a mental health professional. The physician will do this by taking a personal and thorough medical history, order laboratory tests, and perform a physical examination. These tests will provide the mental health professional with helpful information about the specific medical condition that might be causing the anxiety symptoms.

To identify the condition, the psychologist will look at any of the following symptoms difficulty concentrating, difficulty sleeping, muscle tension, irritability, fatigue, restlessness and many others.

What to Do When Your Partner Becomes Anxious?

When this happens, two things may likely occur. Either you start noticing the signs yourself or your partner will confirm to you about their anxiety. Either way, your reaction to this unfortunate issue will have a deep impact on their feelings. Be sensitive about your emotions and reactions to this situation. The things you say and how you say them is very important.

If your partner tells you about their present situation, thank them for trusting you with this vital information. Be empathetic and highly supportive. Don't forget that anxiety is real, it exists. And you need to acknowledge this situation so that you will not end up hurting yourself unnecessarily.

Treatment

Taking a medication to a great extent plays a key role to the treating of anxiety disorders. Research has proven that behavioral treatment, a combination of psychotherapy, with medication will be highly effective. Most times, depression, alcohol dependence and other conditions will have a strong effect on mental wellbeing to the extent that treating anxiety will have to be suspended till all the underlying conditions are adequately controlled.

Self-Treatment

In most cases, a person can treat anxiety at home without seeking for clinical assistance. However, this is not recommended because it won't be effective for long-term or severe anxiety disorders.

There are a host of exercises and actions that will help the patient to remain focused, and cope with shorter-term anxiety disorders such as:

- **Stress Management-** managing your stress level can reduce potential triggers. Learn how to organize your daunting tasks and take some time off from work or study. You need rest periodically.

- **Relaxation Techniques-** engaging in some relaxation activities will help in soothing the physical and mental signs of anxiety. Some of these techniques include yoga, resting in the dark, long baths, deep breathing exercises, and meditation.

- **Replace Negative Thoughts with Positive Ones-** condoning negative thoughts are not good for your mental health. Remove all the negative thoughts from your mind and replace them with positive ones. Confront your fears such as phobia with courage and unflinching determination.

- **Engage in Networking-** connect with familiar and highly supportive people, such as a friend, peer or family member. Network with only those that believe in you.

- **Exercise-** engaging in exercise routine is good for your physical and mental health. It will release 'feel good' chemicals in your brain, and this will trigger positive feelings and boost your self-image.

Counseling

Psychological counseling remains one of the best ways to treat anxiety. This can come in multiple ways including:

- *Cognitive-behavioral therapy (CBT),*

- *Psychotherapy*

- *A combination of therapies*

Practitioners of cognitive-behavioral therapy believe that there is need for patients to limit their distorted thinking, change the way they react to situations or objects that trigger anxiety. This aspect of psychotherapy helps to recognize harmful thoughts that trigger troublesome and anxious feelings.

A Combination of Medications

Some physical and mental symptoms of anxiety can be controlled with a wide range of medications such as benzodiazepines, antidepressants, tricyclics etc.

Benzodiazepines- depending on the condition of the patient, a doctor may recommend benzodiazepines. Patients should keep in mind that they may be highly addictive. Medically, this medication has lesser side effects besides possible dependence and drowsiness.

Valium or Diazepam is few examples of commonly prescribed benzodiazepine.

Antidepressants- this helps to treat anxiety and people suffering from depression. It has lesser side effects, but may likely cause sexual dysfunction, nausea and jitters during the treatment. Other types of antidepressants include Celexa or citalopram, and Prozac or Fluoxetine.

Tricyclics- these are a combination of drugs that could help to treat anxiety disorders. Some of these drugs have side effect such as weight gain, dry mouth, drowsiness, dizziness and lots more.

Commonest examples of tricyclics include clomipramine and Imipramine. Other additional drugs that may be helpful include beta-blockers, buspirone, monoamine oxidase inhibitors etc.

If the adverse effects of these conditions become severe, the patient is advised to seek a medical help immediately.

Prevention

There are many tested and proven ways to limit the risk of anxiety disorders. Keep in mind that anxious feeling can be triggered unexpectedly. Some psychologists believe it is a natural factor of daily life. So, experiencing them is not a sign of mental disorder. Some steps could help to moderate anxious emotions such as:

- *Limiting the intake of chocolate, cola, tea and caffeine.*

- *Before you use any herbal remedies or over-the-counter medication, confirm from your doctor or pharmacist if there are any chemicals that may trigger anxiety disorders.*

- *Eat a healthy diet*

- *Maintain a good sleep routine.*

- *Flee from cannabis, recreational drugs and alcohol.*

Symptoms of Anxiety

Common symptoms of anxiety include:

- *Fear*

- *Uncontrollable worry*

- *A rapid or fast heartbeat*

- *Muscle tension*

- *Difficulty concentrating*

- *Feeling on edge*

- *Restlessness*

- *Tingling*

- *Physical discomfort*

- *Irritability*

- *Shaking*

- *Trembling*

- *Sweating*

Identifying Anxiety Triggers

Yes, you are living with anxious partner, and you may be wondering the best way to identify anxiety triggers. It is important to know that anxiety trigger is unique to every individual.

If you assess different anxiety patients, you will most likely observe that there are lots of common factors. Identifying these triggers can help you to learn the right way to cope with this issue, and also help your partner manage the condition successfully.

The following tips will help you to recognize the anxiety triggers:

Keep a Journal

Keeping record of your activities on paper will enable you to find the best way to analyze what is happening to you. It will help you to observe situations that make you feel anxious. Thus, writing down any effective strategy will be extremely helpful. It will enable you to re-focus and refer back in the future.

Identify Life Stressors

Major stressors such as job change or loss, change of job schedule, complicating relationship issues, death of a loved one, and unexpected pregnancy can result in anxiety. Think about any present stressors that may be triggering your anxiety level.

Reflect on Your Past Experiences

Yes, thinking about the ugly past can trigger anxiety. Desist from thinking about the past; there is no future in the past. Some negative past experiences may still be affecting you today. Think about it, and re-frame your mind.

Talk to a Trusted Fellow

A trusted partner, family member or friend can provide awesome insights on specific situations that could trigger anxiety. If you need additional help, you may consider reaching out to a professional therapist to help you.

Listen to Your Body

Be mindful of what you eat. Alcohol, sugary foods and caffeine are capable of raising your cortisol levels, thereby triggering your partner's anxiety level.

Seeing a Psychologist

Although, multiple factors can trigger anxiety and there are many types of anxiety disorder. According to research, some can be triggered by similar underlying circumstances.

Sometimes, patients try to cope with the negative reactions by making frantic efforts to avoid experiences, situations, and unpleasant feelings that try to trigger anxiety in them. Some could not do this effectively; they end up becoming overwhelmed by their emotions. However, avoidance is not healthy; it can backfire and ultimately fuel the anxiety.

The role of a psychologist is unique; they aid in diagnosing and teaching patients' effective ways of coping with the situation and how to live healthier. An aspect of psychotherapy called cognitive-behavioral therapy (CBT) is helpful in treating the situation.

Seeing a psychologist remains one of the best things you can do to your partner when they are affected with anxiety disorder.

Through cognitive-behavioral therapy, patients understand how their thoughts can lead to anxiety symptoms. By learning the right way to change those thought patterns, they will obviously limit the intensity and likelihood of anxiety symptoms.

Psychotherapy is a collaborative process; here both the psychologist and the patients work in harmony to develop concrete skills, techniques and specific concerns that will help in coping with anxiety.

Besides, cognitive-behavioral therapy, psychologists are well trained to use other approaches to help the patients confront their fears such as 'group psychotherapy', this involves treating different people who have anxiety disorder simultaneously, and providing them with the needed support to navigate the situation.

Family psychotherapy can aid family members to understand their loved ones' anxiety, learn new ways of interacting that do not trigger anxious habits. Family therapy is highly recommended for adolescents and children suffering from the anxiety issues.

Anxiety disorder regardless of the degree is treatable. Many of the people who suffer from anxiety are able to eliminate or reduce symptoms after fewer weeks or months of psychotherapy. Some patients notice maximum improvement and often times get properly healed after few sessions.

CHAPTER TWO

How Anxiety Affects Relationships- The Bad and Ugly

Having anxiety disorder can negatively impact several aspects of your life including your relationship with your partner. There are some tested and proven ways anxiety can lead to problems and as well strategies that can be implemented to navigate those unhealthy patterns.

Being Overly Dependent

Some people with generalized anxiety disorders have a great desire to be close to their partners, friend or family members, depending on them for healing, reassurance and maximum support.

Together with being overly dependent, people with generalized anxiety disorder are prone to over thinking, being indecisive, planning for worst case scenarios, seeking out constant communication and fearing rejection, and even getting more anxious if their partner do not respond promptly.

Combating Problematic Dependency

As a partner, you may not have the required skills to help your beloved navigate through anxiety disorder. You may misunderstand your partner, and this can frustrate your relationships. Give yourself time to think about this process and see if you can regain some perspective.

Then since you are unqualified to handle this situation, and instead of struggling to provide assistance which you are unskilled to give, take your partner to a therapist who specialize in handling anxiety patients and you will be happy you did.

Being Avoidant

Some patients of anxiety disorders try to avoid coping with partners as a way of dealing with the situation. Some may go to the extent of avoiding negative emotions like frustration or disappointment by being vulnerable, not opening up or revealing their true feelings.

A person who is caught in this situation may be described as lacking empathy, emotionally unavailable or cold, even though they may be honestly longing for closeness from loved ones.

Cognitive behavioral therapy and other forms of therapy including psychodynamic psychotherapy can be helpful in combating avoidance. A mental health professional is adequately trained to explore past and present relationships as well as the emotions surrounding those interpersonal communications.

Anxiety can help or motivate people to sense danger within their relationships or environment. Anxiety disorder can be debilitating or overwhelming, and this can be highly detrimental to a relationship.

Be rest assured that getting the right treatment can help the patient develop fulfilling, long-lasting and healthy connections with others.

Required Steps to Managing Relationship Anxiety

Seek for Help

Individual counseling can help to manage your fears in a relationship or take actionable steps towards your partner. Counseling your partner is the first step that could help you navigate this process; it will boost communication and enhance problem-solving skills in the relationship.

Understand Your Interests

What is your sole interest in being part of this relationship? If your overall focus is on a romantic relationship, there are chances that you may be frustrated or even feel anxious.

Building a quality relationship with your partner that exceeds romantic relationship can make your partner to feel better about you and the mental desire to improve. Your partner at this point deserves to know that you love and care for them.

Examine Your Thinking

Sometimes, becoming anxious makes it extremely difficult for you to think whether a worry is legitimate or not. For example, if you are too anxious, you may be thinking that your partner is planning to leave or cheating when there is no evidence to prove that.

You can consider working on managing your anxiety by communicating better with your partner, developing healthy habits, or objectively addressing issues that affect your relationship.

Communicate Your Values

Sometimes your partner may be focused on making you to love and appreciate them only, while forgetting or even ignoring to reciprocate through their actions.

This is the reason why you show them love and affection, you should also courteously communicate your values and needs. Confirmed that compromise is an essential part of every relationship, but this doesn't imply that you shouldn't be assertive or share your thought when something is also important to you. The earlier you communicate your needs and values to your partner, the less likely you will feel resentful.

Don't Avoid

This is one of the worst measures you will take in a relationship. You don't have to distract yourself or avoid the issues that cause problems. Trying to avoid is a temporary strategy that often end in heated arguments.

Set a standard that will aid you to address the issues in the relationship at first, and then if you need a more professional fellow to assist, then don't hesitate to work with a counselor individually or collectively.

What Anxiety Is Doing to Your Partner

Understanding some facts about anxiety will help to support your partner the best possible way. Popular therapist Helen Odessky and erudite psychologist, Dave Carbonell, among other mental professionals recommend that you should keep some of these things in mind:

- Anxiety is a real mental health issue.

- Anxiety is normal. At certain points of life everyone has it.

- It can only become a disorder or a serious issue when it becomes severe.

- It is a debilitating mental illness that prevents one from living a normal life or functioning well.

- It makes people to experience flight or fight reactions to situations that are not life-threatening such as worrying about whether your partner will leave or ever cheat.

- It is not easy to cure or fix anxiety, healing takes a gradual process.

- Most of the people who have anxiety wish they never have it. Some of them also get worried that they are becoming a burden to others due to their anxious lifestyle.

- Millions of people right now are dealing with anxiety and a greater percentage of them are happy with their lives, and relationships. You too, can.

- Patients of anxiety disorder have periods of time or situations when they don't experience the symptoms. This is why many psychologists confirm that the symptoms can occur in waves or both.

- There is no logical or rational reason why people should be anxious. Yet, it causes some patients to worry about situations, even when there is no reason for them to do so. Anxiety can make your partner to act irrationally, even when there is no evidence that they should worry about.

- Anxiety is treatable. It is not a weakness. Psychotherapy remains the best strategy that can relieve symptoms and teach the patient how to cope with it.

How Anxiety Can Influence Your Relationship

When you are in a relationship or dating someone with anxiety disorder. It is possible that your partner will spend a great deal of time ruminating on everything that has either gone wrong or will ever go wrong or that could go wrong in the relationship. Below are some of the thoughts that may be running through their minds:

- *What if my partner doesn't love me as much as I do?*

- *What if they are lying to me?*

- *What if they are hiding something from me?*

- *What if they are cheating me or attempting to leave?*

- *What if they are thinking of cheating on me?*

- *What if they like someone else?*

- *What if my present anxious state ruins our relationship? (Becoming anxious about anxiety).*

- *What if we finally break up? And lots more.*

Some patients of anxiety have few of these thoughts running through their minds. These 'what if's' are normal part of being in a relationship. So, don't be scared about it. Anxious patients tend to have these thoughts more intensely and frequently.Some even get worried of worst-case-scenarios. The anxious thought causes a wide range of physiological symptoms such as:

- *Anxiety attacks*

- *Insomnia, and*

- *Shortness of breath*

Some of the anxious patients will react vehemently to the relationship stress with either a flight or fight response, as if the stress were to be a physical attack. Anxious thoughts can make your partner to act in irrational ways that could strain the relationship.

For example, let's say your partner is anxious because he/ she is the first person to initiate a conversation. They may start to worry or assume that you no longer love them. If this is left untreated, it can intensify their anxiety level, and they may be tempted to think that you may never chat with them if they didn't reach out first.

To resolve this anxious state, your partner feels it is good that you are the first to initiate the communication. Trying to reach out to your partner a few times until they feel comfortable that you always love them and have their interest at heart at all times can heal the situation.

Over the years, I have met and interacted intensely with people who have or are still encountering different anxiety-motivated behaviors in their relationships. Here are a combination of their features:

- Perfectionism

- *Passive aggressive behavior or avoidant*

- *Having trouble focusing and being directed*

- *Being overly critical*

- *Being controlling*

- *Being irritable*

Dating Someone with Anxiety

When you are dating someone with anxiety, there is a possibility that their anxious state will surely affect your social life. You may have issues taking your partner along to all the social gatherings or events you had always wanted to go. This could cause both of you to have heated arguments or even grow apart

How to Cope with the Situation

Don't let anxiety have a negative tag on your relationship. You can build a healthy relationship with an anxious partner. All you need to do is to contribute your quota. You can do this by using the right strategies. Build an amazing relationship and stop anxiety from causing untold stress both to you and your loved one.

Inspire Your Partner to Work with a Therapist

When you are in love with someone with anxiety, you may be tempted to support in any way you can. Yes, that is good and expected. You may even try to act as a surrogate therapist. But the real issue that you are not a therapist. It could be emotionally draining to ever contemplate or think of playing that role. This could make you to resent your partner.

You lack the skills to provide the needed therapy to your partner. This is why it is good you encourage them to consider working with a therapist. Working with a therapist is the best antidote to the situation. They will help them to deal with the situation, both in and outside the relationship.

Working with a therapist can take the pressure off from you and your partner. Don't encourage or allow them to handle their situations by themselves, many can't. In fact, experience has shown that many lack the capacity to do this, even when they have the desire to do so. Desire is not enough.

Working with a Therapist Yourself

If your partner resists your suggestion to consult a therapist, should you leave them? Should this be the reason to end the relationship? Should you take the exit door? Certainly no. You should go for it, consulting a therapist as fast as possible. Going for it will achieve multiple results for you. It will help you to develop the needed skills to know the right way to cope with their anxiety. A therapist will also teach you effective ways of coping and living with an anxious partner. When you are in love with someone with anxiety, it is very easy for you to forget taking proper care of yourself. You need to go for a therapy. This will help you to focus reliably on your mental health.

Communicate Better About the Issue

Really, anxiety is scary. It can de-motivate you to avoid talking about it. One of the most tested and proven ways to cope with anxiety is to talk about it directly with your partner, openly. Having a heart-to-heart chat on what they are feeling right away and how they are feeling it is very important. To show your partner you care and appreciate them, you need to encourage them to openly talk about it. Listen to them attentively without judging them.

In the course of the conversation, try to let them know that you are there for them, and you are ready to help them get healed. Asking them questions like this could help 'what do you think I can do to help with your anxiety?

Managing Your Reactions to the Anxiety

When conversing with your partner about their anxious state, it is easy to become upset or take it personally. Some people may even interpret it as rejection, selfishness or attempt to create a gap. Your overall focus may be for them to get over it. There is a possibility that you may just want them never to worry about it. Don't do this. It will never solve the situation. It will be a counterproductive technique. Thus, you need to turn your reaction into something more compassionate.

Imagine your partner wake up one morning and says he has the feeling that you are cheating. You don't have to take it personally. The moment you start ruminating over this, you will likely going to be upset. You may worsen the situation by saying something that is mean or aggressively react defensively. Never, don't make the matter, even worse.

Instead allowing this situation to escalate your anger, take some time off to calm down your nerves. Don't fight your partner. Remind yourself that your partner is anxious, and this is having an unfortunate impact on them. This is not just about you; it is about your partner. You are not the source of it.

Address your partner in a calmly and loving way. You can begin by saying something like this 'Oh sweetheart, I am sorry you are feeling that way. I can understand your feeling, that must be hard. Is there anything you feel we could do to make you feel better about that?

It is very important you manage your reaction; it will help you to set boundaries and be there for your partner both in good time and bad. It is even more important than managing your partner's reactions.

Set Boundaries

When you are in love with someone with anxiety. It is good to strike a balance between setting boundaries and being patient. Recognize how their anxiety can affect their behavior.

Depending on the situation, and the partner involved, most times it is not always good to be the one that bends. If you always yield to their concerns, you may likely become bitter and resentful towards your partner.

You can set some healthy boundaries by telling your partner with love that certain behaviors are not acceptable even during stressful times and attacks that aggravate anxiety:

- *Threats*

- *Accusations*

- *Insults*

Tell your partner that you are passionately optimistic that they can take meaningful steps to improve or cope with their anxiety. This is part of setting boundaries.

Anxiety causes untold stress both to yourself and your partner. It could evoke fear and anger. Often times we instinctively see it as a problem, nothing more, nothing less.

Some clinical psychologists recommend that couples should always shift their mindset about anxiety. Instead of seeing it as a source of stress, you can be curious about it. Trying to understand how anxiety works, could make you difficult to be angry about it.

Tested and Proven Ways to Support Your Partner

There is a classical difference between serving as your partner's unofficial, unpaid therapist and providing the relevant support. While it is confirmed that a therapist can do so much for you and your partner. It is also important to note that there is a limitation to what a therapist could do. A therapist will not take your partner out for a dinner or go out to watch a movie together or hold their hands, rub their palms, or even kiss them when they attempt to cry.

Anxiety can further hurt or deepen your relationship. Besides being a source of stress in your relationship, it is also a great opportunity to truly understand your partner and love them more deeply.

Seeking for the services of a mental health professional is one of the awesome ways to support your partner and make your relationship become stronger and more fulfilling. These are some of the activities that will make them feel secured and loved. It helps them in getting relieved. Here are some ways you can support your partner:

Acknowledge Their Efforts on Anxiety Issues

If your partner is making frantic efforts to work on their anxiety, please don't forget to acknowledge that. This is why it is necessary you celebrate your partner's strengths when it is possible.

Listen Attentively

Listening attentively is key. Try to listen to them carefully. Be patient while listening to their worries, complains or concerns even when you feel they are saying something you already know. Listening to them carefully and attentively proves to them that you care.

Many people living with anxiety have millions of thoughts going through their minds simultaneously, and many times you see them remain quiet, speechless, helpless and sad. Because they are held down by many uncertainties and fatigue of their daily burden. Often times asking them what's on their minds could be incredibly helpful. If you are willing to provide a listening ear, it would be extremely helpful.

Include Them in Your Mental Health / Self-Care Rituals

If you have any rituals or hobbies that are very good to your mental health, kindly recommend them to your partner. This could be running, walking, breathing exercises, chatting with loved ones, colleagues, peers, friends and family members, listening to relaxing music and much more. If you do any of these, and they have been quite helpful, kindly include your partner.

Research shows that including your partner in any of these rituals can help both of you to limit anxiety in your relationship. If you have experienced anxiety, you can agree on one thing that it is a bitch. Living in constant fears or having panic attacks is not fun.

When you are anxious, you will observe that you are not the only person that suffers because of it- your partner, family, friends, peers, workplace colleagues, and others around you are deeply affected by the mess happening around your heads.

Thus, when you are living with someone with anxiety, know that one of your strongest obligations is to be a good support system to them. You are expected to love and support them.

Anxiety is a common mental disorder that affects a greater percentage of people. Over the years, I have worked with several people who have tried countless things to shut it up including writing, chatting with loved ones, speaking in a familiar environment, eating a healthier diet, engaging in lots of physical and mental exercises, and seeking for a professional therapy.

Anxiety Disorder Doesn't Mean Mentally Deficient or Inferior

Do not see your partner to be mentally deficient or inferior. Anxiety issues are triggered by so many factors especially overly apprehensive behavior. Some sufferers learnt their overly apprehensive behavior either directly or indirectly from their parents or those who raised them or those that had profound influence in their lives.

It is not true that most anxiety disorder patients willingly adopted this unfortunate way of life, as a way of coping or dealing with life, but a greater majority of them adopted this style because they believed it was the right way to live. Some of these people find out later in life that they have issues with anxiety when it begins to cause series of problems in their lives.

To overcome this issue, the patient needs to learn healthy ways of coping with life, by eliminating issues with problematic anxiety. Overcoming anxiety requires getting the right help, support and information, living with a helpful partner and working with the right therapist. Once all these are available, then overcoming anxiety will be achievable.

The road to recovery may not be easy or quick, success is achievable with perseverance and effort. Thus, you don't need to feel sorry for your loved one who is currently struggling with anxiety disorder; all you need to do is to offer support and empathy instead of pity or sympathy.

There Are No Quick Fix Cures or Shortcuts

Anxiety disorder is caused by behavior. To overcome this issue, the patient will need lots of hard work, support and help from an experienced and willing anxiety disorder therapist.

So, there is no short cut or quick fix to it. It is unrealistic to think that a patient can just get themselves out of the situation without doing the needful. With this understanding, it will be easy for you to assist your partner get all the help they deserve. You need to be more supportive as the person works through the process.

Reassure Your Partner That They Will Be Fine

Anxiety is capable of creating one of the strongest emotional, psychological and physiological responses such as tensions, symptoms, sensations and feelings. This is why most anxious patients feel they are losing their minds or in the verge of losing their minds, will break down or even dies.

Although, anxiety disorder is a misnomer, but some psychologists believe that it is enough to cause death, physical breakdown or collapse. Though, this belief is yet to be proven to a logical conclusion. Once the patient calms down, all the strong emotional sensations, feelings, or symptoms will subside or diminish drastically.

So, when your partner is having an episode of high anxiety, it is important you reassure them that they are going to be fine. This will calm their nerves and makes them feel better.

Stay Calm

Most anxiety disorder is triggered by fear; this fear could be rational or irrational. Fear can cause a number of changes in the body both emotionally, psychologically and physiologically. These changes are capable of producing anxiety symptoms. Sometimes, some anxious patients react to these symptoms more than fear itself.

When your loved one is struggling with anxiety, encourage them to remain calm. Once they calm down, they will feel better with time. It may take the body about 20 to 30 minutes to recover from an active stress response.

Encourage Your Partner to Make Healthy Behavioral Change

It is good to be supportive and empathetic, but it is not enough. If your partner is not making the needed effort to seek help, they may remain stuck. Anxiety disorder will get resolved when a person works at it, and most patients seldom makes effort on their own. You should not just be an enabler, but an encourager. Inspire them to seek the necessary help, to work towards making healthy behavioral change.

Support Your Partner to Consult a Therapist

Traditionally, many people have a lame view of consulting a therapist. Happily, this view is changing quickly. So many anxious people are seeking for professional help for emotional, psychological and physiological challenges today than ever before. The main reason is that more and more people are seeing effective results doing this.

If your loved one is thinking of consulting a therapist, please give them all the necessary encouragement they may need and support them as they continues. Overcoming anxiety is not a child's play. It takes time and effort. Encouraging and supporting them in any way you can, will help them to walk through times of discouragement. Lasting success is achievable for those who persevere.

Be Available

Make yourself available at all times. Making yourself available entails showing your loved one that you are 100% ready to talk with them on anything at any time without prejudice or fear of judging them. Also, you need to tell them that you will not change the way you think about them. You are there to support them and they can count on you to make a positive difference in their lives and recovery process.

Don't Patronize, Empathize

Try to be as empathetic, loving and supportive as you can. Anxious people feel so bad about all that is going on their lives. They are not comfortable about their situation, and many of them genuinely want to feel better. They really don't need your sympathy, but they will deeply appreciate your compassion, understanding, dedication and ample time to resolve this mental health condition.

Celebrate Small Victories

Overcoming anxiety disorder takes a lot of hard work, time and energy. During the recovering process, keep on celebrating your partner as they improve or achieve many little victories or steps. Celebrate them. Make much ado about them- it helps their healing process. This will be highly motivational to the patient. For example, meeting the therapist for the first time or attending the first session is a victory in itself, and worth celebrating. Experiencing relief or eureka is another reason to celebrate. Continuing the course with the therapist is another reason to jubilate. Overcoming an age-long fear or animosity is another and so on.

Overcoming anxiety disorder is a process that keeps on unfolding in many little steps. Progress is slow in most people, thus celebrating the small victories can motivate the patient to remain focused. Most people who can't succeed in overcoming anxiety do so, not because they don't want to succeed or can't succeed, but because they give up so easily before any meaningful progress is made.

Encourage Them to Feel Better About Themselves

Low self-esteem is an underlying factor why most people don't overcome anxiety disorder. It is good to boost their emotions. Your affirmations and consistent encouragement can help them to feel good about themselves and feel more positive about life.

Take Suicidal Comments Seriously

Overcoming anxiety involves many back and forth, ups and downs. The road to success is shrouded with total disillusionment and despair. There are times when your loved one feels like giving up on life especially if depression is involved. If this happens, you may often hear them making some suicidal comments. If they are contemplating suicide as a way of ending their struggle. Take it seriously and seek for an emergency help like calling the police if the threat seems imminent. Even if you are unsure whether they meant what they say, you still need to proceed with calling an emergency help, it is better to err on the side of preserving the dignity and sanctity of life.

Continually Offer Help

Your continuous assistance can help your partner get through the crucibles of recovery. Once they have recovered, you will recognize the value of what you have done. As I have consistently mentioned previously, overcoming anxiety requires getting the right support, help and right information and then doing the required work subsequently. Success is achievable for those willing to do the needed work. Your help will surely make a significant impact, especially if you know what to do and how to help.

Don't Trivialize Their Feelings

Even if you absolutely do not understand their feelings or what they are going through. Telling them that the reason for their anxiety is 'stupid' or 'silly' is one of the worst things you can say to them. Yes, you may know that their fears or consistent worries are overly exaggerated or irrational, but that doesn't mean you should not feel their pain or express concern over their feelings.

Empathize with them, just like you would expect a loved one to do to you when you are sad or happy. Your partner will feel better when you try to understand their feelings than trivializing it. Making them feel crazier will make the matter worse.

Be Conscious of Their Triggers

Be sensitive of what terrifies or triggers anxiety in your partner. For example, if you are aware that your partner will develop an instant panic at the sight of a heated argument, then try to take reasonable steps to ensure a heated argument doesn't emanate in your home.

Anxiety and Depression Association of America says that about 8.7% of U.S population is suffering from a specific phobia. So, it is possible that your loved one has a specific thing that terrifies them. Taking reasonable steps to ensure they are mentally relaxed will make both of you much happier, and healthier.

Challenges of Living with Anxious Partner

Living with an anxious partner is usually associated with some level of personal distress. Partners of anxious patients often experience some level of parenting, economic, domestic and other responsibilities such as:

Family Activities

Living with such an anxious partner can often disrupt household routines. You may have to be taking care of family responsibilities such as driving children to school, shopping, cooking, bills and lots more. This can make you to be burned out or overwhelmed.

Finances and Employment

Some people find it difficult to keep or get a job due to anxiety disorder. This can have severe financial repercussions. You may now become the only breadwinner, since your loved one is now indisposed to be working and contribute in paying bills. I want to assure you never to get discouraged when this happens, it may not last long. I understand this could be a stressful one, and one that you may never have bargained for.

Social Life

People with anxiety disorder often times avoid engaging in routine social activities. This may also affect your own social life if you are not liberated, thereby making both of you feel isolated.

Emotional Wellbeing

Your partner may feel sad, angry, bitter, resentful, depressed or scared living with you. Some of them may also feel guilty for dealing with anxiety disorder. These challenges are real and daunting. With proper treatment, people with anxiety disorder can live productive lives that include busy schedules, thriving social lives, and successful careers.

CHAPTER THREE

How to Improve Communication with an Anxious Partner

Communication is an essential key in every relationship. This may sound vague to some people, but it is a reality. Often times, it is easy to inform people how important communication is to their relationships and why they should communicate with each other whether in good time or bad.

But it is often difficult to tell them how to truly communicate. If we were not better informed on how to make this happen, then we will have issues opening the door to healthy communication.

Communication is the art of opening, sharing or conveying ideas and authentic feelings. Talking or speaking with our partner is good. It requires discipline to also learn how to be a great listener.

When we communicate, we express ourselves in a healthy way.

In communication, you are required to dedicate some time listening to your partner. Below are some of the great ways you can communicate better with your anxious partner:

Ask Open-Ended Questions

Communication goes beyond talking about what you will eat in the next meal; instead it is all about digging deep, knowing your partner as much you can. Knowing their feelings, likes and dislikes, the causes of their anxiety and trying to make every conversation a heart to heart chat.

Try to always ask your partner open ended questions like 'how was your day? If they respond with simple answer like 'fine or, good' then, try to ask more open-ended questions. This gives them the opportunity to express themselves further, they will share more.

Remember that not everyone will express themselves very easily.

So, be patient with them if they are not as expressive as you had expected. Some anxious partners set boundaries around their emotions and everyone's boundaries are completely unique. You really need to respect and be mindful of their emotional boundaries. When you respect theirs, they will reciprocate accordingly. Ultimately, the more you connect with each other, the more they will be honest and open with you. Communication breeds honesty and trust.

Pick Nonverbal Expressions

If your partner responds 'my day was fine' with an angry, upset, or irritated tone, then there is more to it. They are feeling something more than meets the eyes. They may be passing through a lot internally but may not be ready or disposed to communicate.

Communication is not just about saying something, how you say them is equally important. Our attitude and tone sound louder than mere words. Honestly, it requires some skill to be able to pick up those nonverbal cues from their facial expressions, body language, hands, eye contact and much more.

You Don't Have to Read Their Minds

Most times you can say what a person may be passing through by looking at them. This is not an easy task. As much as it is good to read a person's mind, you may not be a psychologist, so can't read their minds.

If you are unsure what your partner is feeling, courtesy demands that you ask them gently with love. Don't just ignore the problem, ask them. It hurts their sensibility if you ignore their feelings. It is good to ask them what is going on.

Some partners will be happy to tell you how they feel; they will try to express their feelings in a healthy way. If your partner is passively aggressive, let them know that it is not good for either of you when they aren't honest about their true feelings.

Guaranteed, it is good to read people's minds, but we are humans, and the possibility of making mistakes in our assumptions is high. It becomes a necessity to understand each other and be patient with them, too.

Conversations Are a Two-Way Process

When you are communicating with your partner, it is good you keep in mind the words you use like 'I, you or we'. If the conversation is self-centered, then it is not really a conversation. Remember to make it inspiring by asking them how they feel; their thoughts, ideas, feelings, and what is going on with them.

In a relationship, both of you should have equal opportunity to say things that interests you. It is not just a one-way process. Both of you should feel heard and be able to share your thoughts accordingly. None of you should try to dominate. Having a viable conversation is like playing a table tennis competition, it is something that flows naturally back and forth to each other almost in the same frequency.

Tell Your Partner Your Expectations from Them

Like I mentioned earlier, you are not a mind reader. So, it is essential you keep your partner truly informed so that both of you can be on the same page.

Seeking advice from them when and where necessary can help in alleviating some of the stress or miscommunication in every given situation. Miscommunication breeds unnecessary arguments. At every time, tell your partner you are there for them, and assure them of your unflinching loyalty in perpetuity.

Communication Is a Great Skill

This means that there is ample room for improvement. It is good to work together with your partner, so that you can find out the best way to maintain a healthy relationship with them. You owe it to them to be as thoughtful, kind, direct, and honest as you can.

Know your communication styles. If you are having issues in getting along with your partner, then it can be helpful to familiarize yourself with psychological differences embedded in communication. Counseling psychologists outlines three key communication types such as:

- *The blaming*

- *The explosive*

- *The silent*

All these three can have an influence on your relationship. Each of them is modeled to a person's reaction to a specific issue or conflict.

Try to Validate Their Feelings

There are lots of communication strategies that could cause untold issues such as contempt, stonewalling, etc. But, there is an interesting one, which is often left out of discussions, and that area is validating the feelings of your partner. Validation of feelings means recognizing the emotions whether positive or negative that comes out of your partner, and then attempt to belittle, ignore, minimize or negatively judge these feelings.

If your partner is crying or wailing for example, don't be angry or upset that they are crying or wailing. If they are also feeling positive, don't ridicule their feelings. There are reasons why people have a particular feeling at different times. You can validate their emotions by saying things like 'I can understand your feeling' or 'I see how you are feeling' etc.

Prioritize Kindness

It is always good to treat your partner with courtesy, and respect. Your communication will keep on improving if you don't succumb to the temptation to be bitter or cruel. If it seems that is the best thing to do. Kindness will boost your relationship and ensures its longevity.

Kindness is the ability to appreciate and cherish people more than they ever deserve or can imagine. Lovers that use destructive behaviors during arguments like withdrawing from the discussion, resorting to personal criticisms and yelling are most likely going to break up than couples that dialogue constructively. If for any reason you are angry or upset, take some time off, reflect before you act.

What You Should Not Do

Your partner is suffering from anxiety issues; please try not to make the matter worse by either creating more stress or hurting your partner in the process. Do not:

- *Dismiss their anxiety*

- *Criticize or mock them for having anxiety*

- *Boost maladaptive anxious behaviors by coddling them so much.*

- *Take everything personal*

- *Try to be an unofficial therapist; you lack the training to handle their situations at an advance level.*

- *Lose your temper or flare up whenever their anxiety level escalates.*

- *Recommend drugs for their anxiety, you are not a psychiatrist.*

Nutritional Foods That Relief Anxiety

Research has shown that certain foods guarantee a calming effect. Anxiety symptoms can make your partner feel unhappy, unwell, and unmotivated. Coping with anxiety is not easy. To navigate this process, you will need to make certain lifestyle changes like eating a healthy diet.

Anxiety is characterized by nervousness and constant worry, and often times related to poor health status. Several strategies can be helpful such as:

- *Meditation*

- *Exercising*

- *Deep breathing*

Besides these factors, there are also some healthy foods that can help to reduce the severity of anxiety symptoms, because of their brain-boosting properties. In my practice of working with a host of patients, I have never failed to educate them the great roles diets play in helping to manage anxiety.

In addition to these healthy guidelines are:

- *Drinking enough water*

- *Eating a balanced diet*

- *Staying hydrated*

- *Avoiding or limiting alcohol and caffeine*

There are a host of other dietary considerations that are helpful in relieving anxiety; they help in creating a calmer feeling. A diet rich in fruits, vegetables and carbohydrates remains a healthier option than eating a wide range of carbohydrates in processed foods.

The time you eat is also very important. Skipping meals can make your loved one to drop in your blood sugar level. This can cause you to feel jittery or even worsen underlying anxiety.

Here are tested science-based healthy foods that can provide anxiety relief.

1. Salmon

Salmon is highly beneficial in limiting anxiety. It contains nutrients that promote the brain such as omega-3 fatty acids, docosahexaenoic acid, and vitamin D. It helps in regulating the serotonin and neurotransmitters dopamine, which can help in relaxing and calming properties.

Amazingly, these fatty acids can prevent brain cell dysfunction and limit inflammation that leads to series of mental disorders such as anxiety. Eating adequate volume of salmon can promote your brain's ability to adapt to changes, thereby allowing you to handle stressors that cause or triggers anxiety symptoms.

Try as much as possible to take at least a few servings of salmon weekly. One study observed that men who consume Atlantic salmon three time in a week for five consecutive months experienced less anxiety than those who eat beef, pork, or chicken. Men who ate the later had improved anxiety-related symptoms including heart rate variability and heart attack.

2. Chamomile

This is a helpful herb that limits anxiety. It is composed of high volumes of antioxidants that aids in reducing inflammation, which decreases the risk of anxiety.

Some studies have taken time to examine the relationship between anxiety relief and chamomile. They found out that patients diagnosed with generalized anxiety disorder experienced high reduction in symptoms after eating chamomile extract, than those who did not.

Another study also confirms that people who ate chamomile extract for eight weeks experienced reduced symptoms of anxiety and depression. Currently, there is an ongoing research on the anti-anxiety effects of chamomile tea; many people are consuming this tea in a consistent consistency in different parts of the world. Chamomile is helpful in anxiety reduction due to its anti-inflammatory and antioxidant effects.

3. Turmeric

This spice contains curcumin, which aids in the prevention of anxiety disorders and promotion of brain health. Test tube and animal studies found out that curcumin enhances the omega-3 fatty acids by synthesizing your body and making it to operate efficiently and effectively.

Curcumin has anti-inflammatory and antioxidants properties which help to prevent damage of brain cells. It helps in boosting blood antioxidants levels, which is usually low in people with anxiety.

4. Dark Chocolate

Dark chocolate is helpful in easing anxiety. It contains flavonols which benefits brain function. They boost the flow of blood to the brain and enhance its capacity to adapt to stressful situations. Incorporating dark chocolate to your food will comfort those living with mood disorders.

One study found out that people who eat 74% of dark chocolate two times daily for two weeks consecutively will experience improved levels of hormones associated with anxiety like cortisol and catecholamine.

It also increases high levels of neurotransmitter serotonin, which limits the stress that give rise to anxiety. However, dark chocolate should be consumed with moderation, because it is easy to overeat and high in calories.

5. Yoghurt

If your partner is having an anxiety disorder, then encourage them to include yoghurt in their diet. Studies have found that the healthy bacteria or probiotics seen in some yoghurt can improve various aspects of wellbeing such as mental health.

Probiotics foods promote brain function and mental health by inhibiting free neurotoxins and radicals. Another study observed that people who consume an appreciable dose of probiotic yoghurt daily cope with stress easily than people who took yoghurt without probiotics.

A further research observed that women who consumed about 125 grams of yoghurt twice per day for one month had better functioning of their brain regions that control sensation and emotion. Yoghurt contains probiotics, and this has a calming effect on anxiety reduction and boosting of the brain health.

6. Green Tea

Green tea is very effective. It contains L-theanine, which has a calming effect on anxiety reduction and brain health. It contains epigallocatechin gallate, an antioxidant that boosts the brain health.

7. Dairy Products, Meat nd Eggs

They are high in protein and contain essential properties of amino acids which produces the neurotransmitters serotonin and dopamine, which boosts the mental health.

8. Chia Seeds

This is another good source that boosts mental health. It contains omega-3 fatty acids, which have been found to help people living with anxiety.

9. Bell Peppers and Citrus Fruits

They are rich in vitamin C. They contain antioxidant properties that aid to limit inflammation and prevent damage to the cells.

10. Almonds

Almonds have been discovered to be helpful in anxiety reduction. It contains a greater volume of Vitamin E.

11. Blueberries

They are rich in antioxidants and Vitamin C including flavonoids. They are helpful in improving brain health as well as helps in reduction of anxiety.

How to Respond and Deal with My Partner's Specific Type of Anxiety

Having a partner living with anxiety can be difficult to manage. Find out what specifically triggers your partner's anxiety and encourage them to always avoid those places or activities. As a partner, it may not be easy for you to cope with such situations.

You may find yourself frustrated, angry, upset, disappointed or even sad that your supposed dreams for the relationship has been truncated due to your partner's current anxious state.

You really need to understand their specific type of anxiety and implement strategies that will truly and absolutely support them, without enabling or feeding into their fears.

Educate Yourself about Anxiety

How much do you know about anxiety? It is important that you learn about this, including the types of anxiety there are, the triggers, and their treatment. This will enable you to understand what your partner is going through right now. It has not been easy with them.

As long as your partner's current anxious state is impairing your relationship or reducing their quality of life, it will be ideal to make the relevant changes.

When Your Partner Refuses Treatment

Anxiety is a treatable issue. But your partner may decide never to go for any professional help. If such happens in your case, it is good you consider the reason behind their refusal. For example, they may have tried receiving treatment in the past to no avail.

Maybe they didn't receive the right treatment or psychotherapy. This is why mental health psychologists suggest that you work with a professional that uses cognitive – behavioral techniques. This is particularly helpful when working with people that struggle with anxiety.

If one particular treatment technique did not work, maybe a combination of treatments could work. It could also be possible that your partner took too much at a time and ended up feeling more anxious.

Maybe they may need to approach their treatments differently. The best thing you should do is to be supportive, loving and encouraging so that they can desire to seek help. Living with a spouse that is struggling with anxiety could be stressful for you, too. While this can be a herculean task for you, educating yourself about their anxiety, practicing self-care and setting healthy boundaries amongst others can truly help both you and your partner navigate the relationship.

CHAPTER FOUR

Anger Management: How to overcome it and Get the life of your partner back

Anger management is the easiest and a practical way of controlling your emotions in order to get your life and the life of your loved one back and live a more productive life. The recommendations in this book are based on proven clinical wisdom and research.

Anxiety disorder can be triggered by different things, for instance your emotional state; past experiences and personality trait can play a role in getting you in or out of anger. Irrespective of your situation, you really need to know different anger management tips and how you can use them to your advantage; that is exactly what this chapter is set out to achieve.

Your life will never remain the same after going through the pages of this chapter. Here are some simple strategies that will enable you to overcome your angry feelings and live a happier life.

Reassess the Rage

When anger sets in, you really need to view the situation very well. The same thing that happened to you can still happen to your partner or best friend, and they will exercise a different reaction. You can control the anger by pausing a while and look at the situation again.

Get yourself back by asking yourself these important positive questions would help 'is this situation as bad as am thinking or feeling?' 'Can I view this situation from another person's perspective?' 'Is this situation enough to make me get angry?' 'If this is to happen to my loved one or partner will they react the same way?' and so on.

Break the Cycle

When you are excessively angry, your body produces another cycle of aggression that makes you get angrier. However, psychotherapists suggest that you can break the cycle by engaging yourself with relaxation exercises such as envisioning yourself in a calm state like hanging out with your best friend or partner, going to the beach.

You should employ these techniques anytime you get tensed. Pausing and getting a deep breath about the situation can as well yield more positive results.

Express Yourself

The best way to express your anger is to be assertive, not aggressive says American Psychological Association. If your loved one offends you as a result of their present anxious state, communicate your feelings to them. Communication is very important; until you communicate, you will never be heard.

Never use the word 'You' like 'you are very mad by doing things this way' 'you are very stupid, look at how you are doing things' instead use the words 'I' such as 'I am really worried right now because of the way you did things' 'I am not quite pleased because of your present state right now' 'I felt you could have done things the other way round' and many more. Using the words 'You' will end up escalating the situation and even make the other person to hurt you the more.

Hit the Track

Regular exercises can do the magic. Exercises to a great extent reduce tension in your loved one and helps them to get out of anxiety driven lifestyle. Regular exercises also raise the level of hormone in your body. These hormones put them in a happy mood and also reduce the way they get angry over a slight provocation. You and your loved one can also try yoga or running, but ensure you talk to a psychotherapist or health practitioner before venturing into a new exercise program.

Understanding the Concept of Anger

Anger is a natural emotion we encounter in our daily life experiences. We are likely going to be angry when we react to frustration, threat or criticism. This is a healthy response. It is seen in this case as a secondary response to feeling frightened, lonely or sad. When your loved one becomes excessive angry, it may ultimately affect their thinking- and they may likely going to say or do unreasonable things.

This is one thing they should be very cautious about because anything they say out of anger can never be retrieved and it may have a dangerous effect on our lives. This is the reason why we are encouraged never to utter any word if we are angry, because we are likely going to say what will hunt us in future.

What Is Anger?

What do we mean when we say that someone is angry? Or how do we define anger? American Psychological Association defines anger as something that is:

- *Completely normal*

- *Usually healthy*

- *A human emotion*

But it becomes destructive when it gets out of control. Anger is a mental state of mind that triggers all the levels of adrenaline and non-adrenaline. It also increases blood pressure and heart rate. Anger takes a predominant feeling when someone decides to confront or take action on a threat. It takes over our physiology, cognition and behavior.

Most often, people express anger by making loud sounds, adopting postures, staring and baring teeth. For example, if you trespass over the land of a rural dweller or farmer- his approach to you might be hostile; both his posture and body language may change. The same thing happens when you consciously cross your boundary in your relationship.

What Can Make Your Loved One Angry?

People can get angry as a result of the following factors:

- *Grief*

- *Sexual frustration*

- *Rudeness*

- *Hunger*

- *Tiredness*

- *Withdrawal from some formed habits*

- *Physical conditions like menstrual issues*

- *Mental illness*

- *Physical illness*

- *Alcohol abuse*

- *Injustice*

- *Being bullied or teased*

- *Embarrassments*

- *Humiliation*

- *Traffic jams*

- *Failed relationships or marital breakups*

- *Infidelity*

- *Disappointments*

- *Failure in examinations or other life pursuits*

How Will Anger Create Problems to You?

Anger is capable of making you ill. Psychologists and health experts maintain that when we are angry, our body naturally releases spontaneous stress hormones like cortisol, adrenaline and non-adrenaline. Also, our breathing rate, body temperature and heart rate will increase as well. If you are someone that likes to get angry over a slight provocation, then anger will have a negative effect on your overall well-being.

Further research proves that unresolved or uncontrolled anger can give rise to the following health complications:

- *Acute headache*

- *Backache*

- *High blood pressure or hypertension*

- *Insomnia*

- *Digestive disorders or irritable bowel syndrome*

- *Heart attack*

- *Stroke*

- *Lower pain threshold*

- *Weakened immune systems*

- *Eating disorders*

- *Drug abuse*

- *Alcohol abuse*

- *Lower self-esteem*

- *Self-injury and so on.*

What Is Anger Management?

There are different definitions of anger management. Encyclopedias and dictionaries have different definitions of this concept. We are not going to bore you with those details; instead we are going to give you a simplest definition of the term. Anger management is simply defined as the process of acquiring skills that will help you to control your emotional state when you are angry. It is the art of dealing with your unhealthy situation in a positive way.

If you want to learn how to control your anger towards your partner living with anxiety, then continue to read this book. You will learn healthier tips that will enable you handle the situation.

How to Cope with Anger Management

You can control your anger by engaging yourself with any of the following:

- *Consulting a mental health counselor*

- *Going for anger management course*

Anger management enables you to identify those things that trigger your partner's emotions- it teaches how to talk when you or your loved one is frustrated or infuriated over a situation. When you are angry, you are likely going to say or do things that will make you unhappy or say words or do things that will hunt you in the future.

Signs That Your Loved One Need Anger Management Help

The following shows you need anger management help right away:

- *Their actions are not in conformity with societal laws*

- *They constantly have series of arguments with your friends, partner, colleagues or children*

- *They are always engaged with fights*

- *They frequently hit your children or people*

- *They frequently threaten people with violence*

- *They become reckless while driving*

How to Get Out of Anger

Slow Down

When you are angry, you are expected to devise wonderful strategies that will enable you to slow things down. Try as much as possible to have peace of mind by visualizing a pleasant or relaxing experience.

Express Your Anger

You can express your anger, but ensure you do this only when you have calmed down your worries or nerves. It is best to express one's anger in a non-aggressive way; psychologists say that it would yield more positive results.

Cognitive Restructuring

This is what American Psychological Association (APA) calls changing the way you think or view things. When you are excessively angry with your loved one living with anxiety, make sure you don't use words like 'never' or 'always'- these things tend to make things worse.

Exercise Regularly

Regular exercises help us to diminish the rate in which we get angry. If we engage ourselves with physical exercises- our body will produce better endorphins- natural feel-good hormones.

Do Not Hold to Resentment

When you are angry, ensure you don't hold your grudge against your loved one. Doing so can fuel the situation. Be realistic and have the courage to accept the things you cannot   change.

Learn to Relax

Learning how to relax especially when we are emotionally charged will yield more positive results; it is a requisite skill every angry person should learn. When your mind is relaxed, then you can express your anger in a more productive, assertive way.

Anger management does not mean that you will never get angry. Nobody will expect you not to be angry because you are human. Anger management simply means managing behavioral responses that arise whenever you are angry, especially when this anger was triggered by your loved one living with anxiety. To feel relaxed and calm, take a few moments of your time and relax your nerves.

After this short relaxation session, you will discover that you will never react the way you would have done earlier. This time you will be reacting in a more calm way than reacting out of emotion.

Anger inspires you to fight. You must find a way of discharging this unproductive 'fighting energy or perceived threat'. Due to the ethical and legal constraints of modern civilization, it is extremely likely that when you are provoked, it is possible that your emotions can easily overcome you to the extent that you will verbally attack the other person- your loved one. This happens especially when you feel you have been:

- *Falsely accused*

- *Disregarded*

- *Distrusted*

- *Disrespected*

- *Cheated*

- *Devalued*

- *Violated*

- *Discriminated against and many more.*

In this case, most people crave for revenge. Experience has shown that instant revenge is not really the answer. In fact, revenge will end up escalating the problem more. Try to evaluate the situation in a more productive point of view. Try Engaging in some form of:

- *Meditation*

- *Guided imagery or visualization*

- *Acupressure*

- *Self-hypnosis*

- *Listening to a motivational or inspiring music*

- *Reading your favorite book*

- *Diaphragmatic, deep, rhythmic breathing and so on.*

Reassess the Situations That Provoked You

This is another way to react in a more positive perspective. Find time to reassess the things that actually provoked you. You can start by asking yourself the following questions:

- *Did he or she actually mean to hurt me?*

- *Is there anything I should verify on this situation?*

- *Is this situation really terrible or am I exaggerating the whole stuff?*

- *Do I have concrete evidence that this person intentionally or actually wanted to hurt, antagonize or humiliate me?*

- *Am I taking the whole issue more personal than necessary?*

- *Is there anything I should verify further about this person?*

- *Will it be wise if I react verbally?*

- *Is there anything I can learn from this situation?*

- *Isn't it possible that my loved one's background might be responsible for him or her acting this way?*

The list is endless. Going through what triggers your anger will help you to eliminate it. It can be a catastrophe if you are consumed by anger. Although, there are so many techniques that will tame your anger.

The Root Cause of Anger

It is important to know the root cause of anger if you really want to be angry in more constructive ways. Try to examine any recent setbacks or frustrations that happened to you in the past and know if you ever tried to suppress any of that energy.

Knowing the real cause of anger will help you to handle the situation in a more assertive way. Develop more self-awareness; this will surely free you from this addiction. The best time to evaluate your anger is during the time of relaxation.

At the end of the day, as you lay on the bed, try to replay all the things that happened to you during the day. Examine your conscience and know if you had acted the right way. If you didn't do the right things, try to learn from the experience and do the right things accurately and conscientiously.

Stop Getting Angry

Below are some of the things that aggravate angry feelings:

- *Clenching your fists*

- *Gritting your teeth*

- *Pounding on a couch or desk*

- *Raising your voice and so on.*

According to psychologists, all these physiological responses can make you to get angrier. The more you express your angry feelings, the angrier you become. To get yourself out of this mess, avoid all occasions that escalate angry feelings. Pounding on objects or shouting at the other person ends up making you get angrier.

Do not use any inflammatory language, shake your fist or raise your voice. You will break the addiction that makes you angry by practicing the methods you learnt from a psychotherapist.

Constructive Ways of Handling Angry Feelings

Anger when it is handled in a constructive way will provide better results. When anger is used constructively, it will:

- *Motivate people to express themselves with less apprehension and greater confidence*

- *Improve the quality of life.*

Keep in mind that constructive communication is very important, it is not a debate. Don't expect the other person to read in-between the lines. Avoid occasions that may introduce nit-picking and prior judgments.

Show respect and be tactful, forgive and let go. He, who cannot forgive, will find it difficult to live a healthier, happier life.

Overcoming Explosive Anger

Overcoming explosive anger is another productive way of dealing with your frustration. Some people also call this 'violent outburst'. This simply means handling the situation in a more harmful way. This is the worst thing you can do to yourself.

Overcoming explosive angry is a step in the right direction. Do you get frustrated when your partner or loved one refuses to cooperate with you? Explosive anger will really have a dangerous effect on your overall well-being and relationships.

Explosive anger is an explosion of charged energy. Some people have tried several times to suppress their explosive angry feelings, yet the problem is never resolved.

How to Overcome Explosive Anger

Explosive anger can damage both your physical and mental health and your relationship with the other person. Uncontrolled anger can create other problems like mental disorder. It is important you calm yourself down together with those around you.

The following tips will help you:

Take a Break

Once you discover that you have been caught up with the cobweb of explosive anger, then all you need to do is to stop whatever you are doing, overcome what is irritating you and take a deep breath.

Remember that you don't need to respond to all situations. Give yourself additional time to think about the situation. You can say, 'let me think about it and get back to you' that additional time enables you to cool off. Next time when you will be reacting to the situation, you will discover that you don't need to be explosive. You can now react in a non-aggressive way.

If someone annoys you in your workplace, simply go to your office and think about it. Don't react immediately. Honestly, it takes courage to be able to do this thing.

If someone upset you at home, go to a quiet place like the bathroom and think about the whole situation. You can also take a walk with another trusted person maybe a sibling, business colleague, mentor or peer or someone that can be of great help to you. It is perfectly natural to feel angry over a bad situation but allowing yourself some time off will help you to move on.

Breathe Deeply

Deep breathing is one of reliable ways of controlling your emotions. It is better you say nothing at the hit of anger and take just a deep breath. According to psychologists, taking a deep breath can help you to regain control.

Engage in Positive Self-Talk

Changing the way you think about a particular situation can be of great help. This is known as cognitive restructuring. You can deal with anger in a healthy way by cognitive restructuring. Give yourself some moment to calm down, and then discuss the situation with yourself in relieving and positive terms.

Share Your Thoughts with a Trusted Person

Sharing your thoughts with someone you can trust can be of great help- it can be a great way of venting your anger. Express in clear terms what you had wanted from the other person. The other person will be sympathetic and will surely offer some help advice or solution.

Engage in Physical Activity

The endorphins that come out from your body will help you to calm down when you are caught with explosive anger. If you are a good sports person, there is a possibility that you won't get angry so fast. The following exercises can help you in controlling chronic anger:

- *Weight training*

- *Jogging / running*

- *Yoga*

- *Cycling*

- *Martial arts*

- *Basketball*

- *Dancing*

- *Boxing*

- *Wrestling*

- *Meditation*

- *Swimming.*

Take Enough Sleep

According to mental health experts, adults need about 6-7 hours of sleep every night, so as to function effectively during the day. If you fail to take adequate sleep, it will affect the way you manage your emotions. So, taking enough sleep will lessen your anger and also improve your mood.

Consult your physician immediately if you are guilty of chronic sleep problems. You can also try taking medicinal or herbal supplements to improve your sleeping habits.

Attend Anger Management Class

Attending an anger management programs will help you to overcome anger. When you attend the group class, you will see other people who are facing the same issue with you. You will see that you are not the only one in that situation. You will observe others whose partners are living with anxiety disorders

To get anger management program that is the best for you, all you need to do is to search online or you can ask those that have suffered from the same problem. Look for a group that is tailored to your specific situation.

Consult a Mental Health Expert

If the anger has escalated to the extent that it is interfering with your daily activities, then you should see a therapist. He or she will examine your problem and then know if you need medication, therapy or a combination of the two. A therapist can help you develop communication training and emotional coping skills.

Explosive anger makes it difficult for you to concentrate. It is a secondary emotion to depression, grief, fear, sadness and hurt. Suppressing angry feelings will have a negative influence on your person and relationship with others.

Anger can be both healthy and unhealthy. Thus, you need to deal with the problem of angry feelings through professional or self-help.

Important Tips

- *Watch out the things you say when you are angry- you will realize that after calming down and reflecting on the situation, you will discover that you would have done things the other way round.*

- *Try to listen to soothing music that will guarantee ultimate peace of mind to you.*

- *If you are the type of person that get angry easily, try as much as possible to find a quiet place and think about the situation*

- *When anger sets in, realize that you don't need to lash out at others; you can overcome it by other productive ways we have outlined above.*

- *Block all occasions that aggravate angry feelings on you.*

- *Walk away from the scene if your anger is trying to become violent.*

- *Anger is never a reason to abuse the other person verbally or physically.*

Top 10 Ways to Tame Your Anger

You can tame your temper by engaging yourself with the following 10 anger management tips:

Think Before You Talk

One mark of a great person is the ability to think before they speak. Do not talk at the heat of anger no matter the level of provocation from your anxious loved one, because you are liable to say things that you will regret later. Find some time to recollect your thoughts before you say anything. Also, give those involved in the situation to do the same thing. Stop giving people the opportunity to hate you.

Express Your Anger When You Are Calm

Even though, anger is a normal human activity. Make sure you express it in a non-confrontational, assertive way. State your needs and concerns more clearly without controlling or hurting anyone.

Do Some Exercises

I have talked about this previously. Physical activity is one of the easiest ways to reduce stress. If you feel you are getting angry more than required, go for a walk or spend some time doing things you love or engage yourself with meaningful activities.

It could be hanging out with your friends, chatting with your kids or anxious partner or reading your favorite. Reading is a great way of exercising your thoughts and enlarging your mind.

Take a Time Out

Giving yourself some breaks occasionally will make you release some stress, especially those times you are highly stressed in the office. A quiet moment off from your busy schedule will help you feel better.

Identify Possible Solutions

Don't just focus on what made you mad. Try as much as possible to resolve the issues. For example, if your partner is always late for dinner. Then you can schedule to eat the meal with him at a more appropriate time or you can agree to be eating the meal a few times a week. Don't forget that anger will never fix a problem; instead it will make the situation worse.

Be Respectful and Specific

When you are referring to a situation, try to be respectful and specific. Avoid using hateful words, instead use helpful words. No matter how sad you are, don't abuse the other person. Respect the dignity of his or her person.

Don't Bear a Grudge

Forgiveness is a very important tool; it is something we can use at all times. Alexander Pope once said that to err is human, while to forgive is divine. Don't allow your anger to swallow up your positive feelings for your loved one.

There is joy in forgiving someone that angered you. When you forgive, it means that both of you have learned from the situation. Forgiveness is necessary because everyone will never behave the way you do.

People grew up in different cultures and civilizations-
and these things to a great extent affect the way they
carry out their activities.

Release Tension with Humor

Experience has shown that one can release humor by
lightening up. Humor can make you happy. You can
also find any humorous material and be reading
through it. I have met so many people who usually
read humorous sayings or stories whenever they are
angry. About 80% of them have confirmed that they
release tension shortly after reading through the
articles.

Practice Relaxation Skills

Whenever anger sets in, try as much as you can to put
relaxation skills to work. Imagine any relaxation scene
you have experienced or any one you would like to
experience in future. You might also write few
articles, short poems, listen to music, or do anything

that usually makes you happy. In fact, this is the right time to do anything that encourages relaxation.

Know When You Need Help

Anger management is a big task and a challenge for almost everyone. If you are someone that have tried all the above-mentioned ways and it doesn't seem to work, then consider seeking help from a mental health counselor. If your anger is out of control, you are likely going to do things you will regret later.

Psychotherapy is the treatment of mental situations through psychological methods. If your anger is always destructive or explosive, then you really need to attend an anger management class today.

The role of the psychotherapist is to utilize suggestion, persuasion, insight (self-awareness, perceptiveness), instruction and reassurance during the process of counseling. The sole aim is to make you a better person. There are different types of psychotherapy namely:

- *Interpersonal therapy*

- *Cognitive therapy*

- *Family therapy, and*

- *Psychodynamic therapy*

Depending on your situations and needs, the class may go on for a few hours, few days, a few weeks, and a month and sometimes may last longer. If your loved one have other mental problems like drug addiction or depression, then anger management session will be added to any other treatment you or they may receive.

For proper direction and assistance, make sure that the psychotherapist is aware of your medical history. You will be doing a great disservice to yourself if you fail to reveal your current medical records to the psychotherapist.

Below are some of the aims of anger management session:

- *They help you to identify things that always make you angry*

- *They assist you in responding in a non-aggressive way to those triggers*

- *They teach you how to utilize and acquire specific skills that will help you in handling your anger*

- *They correct your thinking and help you to identify those moments when your thoughts are not leading to rational and logical conclusions.*

- *Teaches you how to experience peace of mind when the anger is surging out.*

- *Teaching you how to respect yourself and others and how to act in a non-aggressive way.*

- *Teaches you how to detect problems and solve them rather than engaging yourself in*

Takeaway Message

Anger affects all aspect of your life both emotionally and physically. All through this chapter, the techniques are presented in a step-by-step, clear format. It offers manageable, real strategies that will help you to control anger.

CHAPTER FIVE

Self-Care Tips When You Love Someone with Anxiety

Loving someone with anxiety is a struggle; you are most certainly struggling with a series of emotions, and questions. Building a stable, loving relationship remains the best antidote. It can feel complicated, when you are in a relationship with an anxious partner.

When anxiety strikes, it can magnify the issues a hundredfold, thereby obstructing the smooth running of your mental state. If you have an anxious partner, you don't have to feel embarrassed about it. There are millions of people out there who have anxiety disorder together with depression.

Anxiety disorder is a common mental illness around the globe. You can actually help your partner become better, do more and achieve more with love, tolerance and understanding. Take some time yourself and reflect. You need time to safeguard your body, spirit and mind.

Over the years, as I have mentioned repeatedly above, I have seen people try the following tips:

- *Engaging in various forms of physical and mental exercises*

- *Eating a healthy diet*

- *Getting enough sleep*

- *Spending quality time in nature*

- *Getting involved with relaxation strategies*

- *Staying socially connected*

- *Getting involved in activities and hobbies they enjoy.*

All these have been extremely helpful.

Here are some of the <u>self-help tips</u> you can do to support yourself and your loved one.

Get Support and Be Supportive

When your loved one is depressed, it can make you to feel upset, angry or frustrated. But, try as much as you can not to allow these feelings to fester and grow. Support groups, counselors and therapists aren't there only for people with anxiety disorder.

You can feel supported; live better and healthier if you seek professional help. This could make you aware of your emotional needs. Therapy will provide answers to all the questions you may have about coping with an anxious partner.

If for some obvious reasons you didn't engage the services of a mental health professional, it is also important you reach out to your support network during this difficult moment.

If loud concerts, caffeine, alcohol, or crowded events trigger your loved one's anxiety, then be supportive and assist them to avoid these things. Try as much as possible to suggest alternatives. Do not pressurize them into doing something that they won't feel comfortable with.

Be There for Them

Your partner deserves your time, love, affection and assistance. Verbalize your support by being there for them. Hold them close to you; listen to their heartbeats while they share their feelings and dreams. Offer the needed help to them. Get involved with some of the daily works they are struggling with. Let them know that you are always there for them, especially during this recovery process.

Don't Take It Personally

Suffering from anxiety disorder can make people to behave in ways they ordinarily wouldn't have done if everything is fine. They may become emotionally withdrawn, irritable, and angry. They may not be interested in doing things or getting involved with things they were used to.

Anxiety is no one's fault. When you are struggling with it, don't abuse them or feel defensive or feel because you did something wrong to them. It is a mental issue. There is no need to take it personally.

Your partner may lose interest in chatting with you or even reduced sexual feelings. Don't take these things personal, it doesn't mean that your partner doesn't love and appreciate you. They are signs that your partner needs treatment.

Help in Domestic Chores

Just when someone is sick or suffering from other illnesses, they may not feel disposed to take care of the house- cleaning the house or paying the bills. Doing some of the daily chores until they are disposed to do them will be ideal.

Treatment Is Important

Treatment is essential to a person's recovery process. You can assist your partner by keeping up with their appointments and taking their medications. Help them to know that seeking for help is not a sign of weakness or even something to be ashamed of.

Offer Hope

Inspire them to be hopeful by reminding them their reasons to keep living- whatever this may be. It could be a beloved pet that needs them always, their amazing children, or even their faith. Find out those things that are unique to them and encourage them to hold tenaciously to it until the pain subsides.

Show Love and Affection

Although, they may be emotionally withdrawn, still don't give up on them, be there for them. Anxiety disorder can make a person to feel unworthy of love, support and feel like a burden. Counteract those thoughts by showing them that you truly love and care for them.

Let them know that you are aware anxiety is affecting their behavior, feelings, thoughts and that you still love them, and will always do. Reassure them that you are here to offer all the support they may need in their journey to get healed and feel better.

Get Informed

Taking some time to find out the real meaning of anxiety disorder and your loved one's unique experience about anxiety such as triggers, how it started, and treatments would be helpful. It will help you to deal effectively with the situation and show how much you love and appreciate them.

Put a Smile on Their Faces

Make them smile. Sometimes always putting a cute smile on their faces will brighten their days. Smile is a medicine. A sense of humor is priceless and highly valuable. You don't have to be serious at all times.

Be Positive

Focus on the positive and don't make your loved one's anxiety the centre and/ or the source of your relationship. Be hopeful that someday soon, your partner will be free from all forms of anxiety.

Inform Them How Much You Love Them

Your anxious partner needs a consistent reassurance that you love them. You may have said 'I love you' today more than five times. But, if your partner needs to hear this for over ten times, please don't need them that privilege.

Just Be There Physically and Mentally Present

Developing a committed, loving and stable relationship speaks volumes. This is one of the best things you can do to your partner. Sometimes saying 'I love you' may not be enough; you need to match your words with actions.

Focus on the Type of Self-Care That Recharges You

Self-care tips vary from one person to another. So, it is important you choose what nourishes you and makes you feel good. Determine the type of activities that makes you feel complete, and pay attention to what makes you feel supported and eases your tension instead of what makes you feel dull or distracted.

Be creative and find out new ways to care and nurture yourself. Remember that self-care is a simple process that could involve breathing deeply and taking a glass of cold water.

Make Your Self-Care a Top Priority

To some people, this might sound selfish or even seem impossible when your partner is in deep emotional trauma or pain. Your primary responsibility is tending to your physical and mental wellbeing and health.

If you don't tend to your own needs, you may have issues with giving your partner all the necessary support they may need. Find out the things you need to relax, nourish, and refresh regularly and then create time for it.

Be Responsive, Not Reactive

When your partner is in turmoil or pain, all you need to do is to practice calming down and finding what you need to do. Pause and take a deep breath. Then ask your partner how you could support them. If they have no idea how you could help, consult a mental health professional.

What to Do When Anxiety Takes Over Your Partner's Concentration

Is anxiety affecting you or your partner's concentration right now? Anxiety has the capacity to send you into a true tailspin of irrational and disruptive thinking that can have a negative effect on your ability to focus.

Anxiety causes a huge stress on your body and brain, thereby sending lots of rush hormones to your body.

When they are released into your body, your heart will beat fast, heart rate will rise sporadically, and your blood will be diverted to limbs to the brain.

When your partner is in this state, their intellect and perception will be clearly impaired, and making it difficult for them to concentrate on their task. So, they need someone like you around them, who can steer them away from anxiety and enable them to gain clarity and concentration.

When anxiety affects their concentration, you don't have to give up on them. Instead, try the following:

Take a Break

If they are working on a project, they can try scheduling breaks every two hours with a timer. They should use the break to practice mindfulness techniques, chat with a colleague at work, speak to you over the phone, and take a walk to reset and much more.

Reduce Caffeine

Taking a cup in the morning may keep you going but having excessive intake can frustrate your ability to focus and work. It can make you a jittery mess.

Speak Positively

They should learn how to adjust their self-talk and make inspiring internal statements and desist from making de-motivational statements like 'I'm hopeless' and 'I can't focus'. Statements like this will only worsen their anxiety level. They should adjust their self-talk to something like 'I need a break, and it is normal to focus'

Take a Deep Breath

This is the best time to get in touch with their breathe. Deep breathing can relieve anxiety in some people. Some psychologist's advice patients of anxiety disorder to practice breath-synchronized movement. Ask them to lift up their hands and exhale deeply.

Tune into Their Senses

They should reset their brain by closing their eyes. Ask them to take a couple of minutes to get in touch with what they touch, feel, smell, see (internally), and hear.

Remind them that lack of concentration is a temporary act. Inspire them and let them know that anxiety is temporary- it comes and goes the same thing with concentration. Reset and recharge with some self-care tips. It is confirmed that anxiety affects concentration, they can overcome it. They have the capacity to do so.

Talk to a Professional

This is an important step that will help your partner to cope. Many of us are dealing with anxiety issues in different ways. Some of us just blow it off, and don't want to discuss it because we want to be perceived as being 'neurotic'.

However, the fact remains that many of our partners are suffering from various degrees of anxiety disorders. The situation is so real than you can imagine. A mental health specialist will help you in dealing with the issue effectively.

Depending on the situation, seeing a psychiatrist will be extremely helpful. They will give you medications that can help to stabilize their moods. Medications play a great role in managing anxiety.

Talking with a therapist and taking medication will help in managing the situation. When you meet a therapist, they will help in developing behavioral interventions that could prevent and/ or manage anxiety.

Don't Suppress Anxiety

Instead of suppressing anxiety, the best thing to do is to learn how to cope with the situation. Anxiety is not something that can just go away. No one has ever succeeded in getting off their minds.

Suppressing anxiety is like expecting your body never to get hungry for two days after you must have eaten to your fill. Anxiety is a necessary emotion. One of your goals should be to identify 'unnecessary anxiety', learning to cope and minimize it as well as developing the mechanisms that will aid in handling it.

 Tell your loved ones to get their minds off the things that make them anxious, and go through life with strong determination, focus and courage. Courage is a great principle of breakthrough.

The most effective way of managing 'unnecessary anxiety' is through preventative measures (meditation and engaging in regular exercises).

How Meditation Can Actually Transform the Brain

I have talked about how meditation helps in managing anxiety issues previously. Here, let's talk about it can truly and absolutely change the brain. Brain is the most important organ of the body. Various scientific and health related studies have proved that it has successfully produced measurable changes to the brain.

The brain and meditation have been a contending issue for some years now. Every new week, new studies keep on coming out to describe some new benefits of meditations. Multiple studies suggest that brain relieves the subjective levels of depression and anxiety, improve concentration, attention as well as psychological wellbeing.

It Preserves the Aging Brain

People who meditate have better preserved brains than those who don't meditate as they age.

It Relieves Activity in the Brain

A recent study at Yale University observed that mindfulness meditation reduces activity of the default mode network. The human brain is responsible for self-referential and mind-wandering thoughts. The default mode network is active when you are not thinking about anything specifically or when your mind is just wandering from one place to another.

Mind-wandering is associated with worrying, ruminating, and being less happy about the past and imaginary future.

Meditation Rivals Antidepressants for Anxiety

A study at Johns Hopkins University analyzed the relationship between mindfulness meditation and their capacity to reduce symptoms of pain, anxiety and depression. According to the researcher, Madhav Goyal and his amazing team, the effect of meditation was moderate.

Meditation is an active form of training the brain. Many people have this view that meditation is all about sitting down one place and doing absolutely nothing. But, Goyal believes that this is not true.

When we talk about meditation, we are talking about training the mind actively to increase different forms of programs. Meditation is not a quick fix or active bullet for anxiety, instead it is one of the effective tools that can help in managing anxiety symptoms.

It Can Lead to Changes in Key Areas of the Brain

A study carried out by Sara Lazar in 2011 and her team at Harvard observed that mindfulness meditation has the capacity to change the structure of the human brain. For eight weeks, they were deeply involved in this study, and the results confirms that mindfulness-based stress reduction enhances cortical thickness in the hippocampus, this governs memory and learning in some areas of the brain, and this helps in self-referential processing and emotion regulation.

Their study also observed that decreases in the brain cell volume are responsible for stress, anxiety and fear. Meditation does not just change the brain, but it also changes our subjective feelings and perception also. In fact, further studies by the same team confirm that meditation training helps in improving psychological wellbeing and mood.

Meditation Improves Concentration and Attention

Having issues concentrating in a task is not a child's play. It affects millions of people whether they do diagnosis or not. Interestingly, improving concentration and attentions remains one of the key benefits of meditation. A study proves that a week of meditation training boost memory and enable people to focus. This means that meditation boosts people's cognitive abilities on the job, too.

It Reduces Social Anxiety

Today, many people are meditating because of its ability to reduce stress, and there is so much evidence that validate this claim. It minimizes a person's stress level both physically and mentally. It serves as a relief to varied symptoms of social anxiety.

It Can Help with Addiction

A greater number of studies have proved this, considering its verifiable positive effects on the self-control regions of the human brain. Meditation can be extremely helpful in assisting people to recover from different types of addiction.

One study confirms that people who engage in meditation were many times more likely to quit smoking faster than you can ever imagine. It helps to de-couple the art of craving for smoking. Meditation is helpful in treating varied forms of addiction.

Meditation Helps Kids to Perform at an Optimal Level

Meditation is effective to physical and mental health and highly recommended for developing brains. There is an increasing interest from researchers and educators in bringing yoga and meditation to school children, especially those that are dealing with the normal stressors inside school, additional trauma and stress outside school. Many schools around the world are happy implementing meditation in their everyday schedules, and the results have been amazing.

Takeaway Message

Meditation is not a complete panacea, but lots of evidence has proved that it is helpful to people that practice it daily and at least twice every week.

Many blue-chip corporations like Apple and Google are integrating meditation in their daily life activities. Meditation is not harmful, instead it is highly beneficial. Certainly, it is worth giving it a shot.

During your leisure either in the morning or evening hours or both, instead of going online, glancing from one page to another or pressing your phone endlessly.

You can achieve great results by quieting your mind by paying undivided attention to your thoughts, listening to the inner visions of your minds, and ruminating over them. A few minutes of meditation can work wonders and make a huge difference in your life and the life of your partner.

Fascinating Things Anxiety Does to the Brain

Anxiety is a common mental illness, which can have a negative influence on your brain. According to the available source from Anxiety and Depression Association of America, about 20% of Americans are suffering from this mental condition. It is described by many schools of thoughts as Americans most common illness.

Although, it is a common mental issue, many people are unaware about its impact on the brain. Anxiety remains one of the surest ways the brain tells us there is an imminent danger. If the brain thinks there is a danger, it will trigger the release of hormones. This includes cortisol and adrenaline.

When the pressing issue is over, the hormones will go back to their normal state. Anxiety can make the patient to feel threatened, thereby leading to the release of excess hormones. Stress can make us to react to dangerous situations. Anxiety can impact our brains in an unexpected way.

Here are fascinating things anxiety does to your brain:

It Influences the Short-Term Memory

If your partner is at any point is feeling forgetful, then there is a scientific explanation to that effect. Increased cortisol will shrink the hippocampus, which some psychologists regard as the 'memory Centre of the brain'.

The effect of anxiety on the hippocampus is fully documented. Thus, an anxious person can become confused and forgetful, and typically this happens when the person is suffering from chronic anxiety, and not occasional mood swings or periods of stress.

It Can Make the Patient Feel Impulsive

When anxiety strikes, it can make the patient to make snap decisions due to the effect of cortisol on the prefrontal cortex- the part of the brain that enables one to make decisions. This can lead to irritability, poor decision making, and impulsive behaviors.

So, if your loved one is feeling anxious, it might be an awesome idea to discourage them from making any big decisions. Because they are not in their best moods, so their decision making process is impaired.

It Can Lead to Symptoms of Depression

Depression and anxiety are two conditions that go hand in hand with. It has the capacity to lead to symptoms of depression faster than you can imagine.

Usually, depression is triggered by anxiety disorder, and the most recommended treatment to this condition is primarily psychological counseling. If you are having issues to cope with anxiety or symptoms of depression, the best thing to do would be to seek professional help.

Anxiety Can Be Influenced by How Your Partner Was Raised

A lot of noticeable factors determine when a person is suffering from this mental condition including environmental, genetic and others. Some popular studies in child development say that the way a person is raised could play an important in their anxiety level.

Further studies prove that nurturing mothers have children with wonderful cortisol receptors, which dampen the stress response, while negligent or insensitive mothers raise babies that become more sensitive to stress in life.

These are known as 'epigenetic changes. The implication is that they influence the way genes are expressed without changing the real genetic code. One person's stressful experiences can affect others along the line, so they can actually be passed down from one generation to the next.

It Can Lead to Insomnia

Many anxiety patients get anxious at night and find it extremely difficult to sleep. Anxiety is one of the verifiable causes of insomnia. It activates the nervous system, thereby altering the brain waves, breathing and heart rate. This in turn affects both the duration and quality of the patient's sleep.

Other symptoms include breathing rapidly, increased heart rate, and feeling nervous. So, anxiety is not just in their heads, there are some scientific reason why many people experience sleepless nights, especially when they are battling with anxiety.

It Can Influence Serotonin Levels

Serotonin is one of the 'feel good' chemicals in the body. It boosts the desire to socialize, sleep, digestion, appetite, sex-drive, aggression, memory, mood and lots more. Thus, if there is an imbalance in a person's serotonin levels, it will affect their mood.

A recent study from University of Cambridge confirms that many people are at a greater risk of depression and developed anxiety because of the way their serotonin transporter gene relate with the environment.

It impacts the amygdala

For people living with anxiety disorders, the amygdala helps to store and process emotions. The amygdale is extra sensitive. It overacts to situations that are inadvertently triggering and threatening the brain circuits that confront an emergency stress response. Two parts of the brain are hugely affected by anxiety are the hippocampus and the amygdala.

What Happens in The Brain When Someone Is Stressed Or Anxious?

The hippocampus and the amygdala are two parts of the brain that aids in the production and processing of anxiety. The hippocampus encodes threatening messages into memories, according to National Institute of Mental Health.

The amygdala is the communication hub of the brain. It is an almond shaped structure that processes incoming sensory signals and interprets them as well. It can alert the brain if a threat is present, and trigger anxiety response or a fear including very distinct fears such as flying, spiders, snakes, dogs and so on. Whenever the brain gets signal of a threat whether perceived or actual, it will release a surge of chemicals like norepinephrine and cortisol. These chemicals give the body a natural boost in speed, perception and reflex time. They can make stimulate the heart to pump faster so that it can get more oxygen and blood circulating through the body.

How Your Anxious Partner Can Boost Their Concentration at Work

Prioritize Tasks

Your partner can improve their focus by handling or tacking complex jobs first and attending to the smaller stuff later. They should create a scale of preference of their tasks and do the most important tasks first. Their topmost priority or 'A list' should include jobs with pressing deadlines of today or tomorrow.

The 'B list' can consists of jobs that needs to be completed within one week, while the 'C list' can include checking your email, replying to some text messages, checking and replying messages from your social media pages. Failing to prioritize tasks can lead to distractibility and complex organizational issues.

Corral Your Email

Focus is key; if you are not focused, you could easily be distracted. Even the most efficient professionals can be led astray by consistent pinging of incoming emails. If your partner is prone to distraction, these incoming signals can derail their whole day.

Instead of reading emails as they receive the notifications, it is important they set out specific time to read and reply to these emails. This has been very helpful to most patients. Encourage your partner to desist from being a slave to always checking their missed calls and emails, especially during their peak working hours.

Reduce Other Distractions

Your partner should learn how to limit unnecessary distractions from their workplace such as having unnecessary conversations with colleagues during work hours, persistent voice mails and away from work. It is always effective to set particular times to check and answer voice messages.

Smash the Work into Smaller Bits

If your partner is becoming overwhelmed, stressed or anxious by the volume of work or if they are spending so much time on a particular task, no matter the type of work that is making them to feel this way. What they should do is to break the work into smaller bits. Then, take the work one step at a time; slowly they will accomplish great tasks.

For example, if they are anxious of writing a report before the end of the week, they shouldn't give up or feel discouraged. Instead, they should break it down into smaller bits, so that they can feel focused. Tell your partner to set realistic goals, and take it gradually, one step at a time or even make sincere efforts to accomplish the tasks, one day at a time.

Work in the Same Place

Working in the same place or location will help your partner to accomplish much. Working in the library today, tomorrow at the office, yet next tomorrow at a friend's place can make them to become super vulnerable or distracted by external stimuli.

When they are acclimatized with an environment, their mental state will get used to that place, and this can actually make them to work better, and perform great task. The takeaway message here is to be consistent with their environment and make efforts to make at the same place at the right time. This will surely increase their natural tendency to work in the location.

Find a Serene Place to Work

The ideal place to work is in a private office, but in today's world, this is not always feasible. Because, most corporations have Dilbert-like cubicles for their employees. If your partner doesn't have their own private offices, there are great ways they can reduce distractions even while in small cubicle.

If your partner is sharing their workspace, it would be ideal if they can share it with someone that doesn't do more of phone work. Someone that does more of computer work could be effective.

Set a Timer

Using a timer and setting it to go off at specific times can make a wandering mind to return to normalcy. When it is off, your partner can continue their task and make sincere efforts to accomplish their A-list projects. During their off task, could serve as an ample opportunity to continue what they were doing.

De-Clutter Their Workspace

Having a serene, sparkling and conducive workspace can help in boosting organizational productivity and focus. But they shouldn't forget that moving items on their desk could be a double edged sword. De-cluttering your workspace is the real deal. So that they won't spend the time they would have used in working to cleaning their desk.

If it becomes expedient that you have to clean your desk, ask yourself what you are trying to do, be honest with yourself, and know if that is exactly what you need right now.

Use a Personal Digital Assistant

Tell your partner to use a personal digital assistant or a day planner, this will help them to be more productive and efficient. This will be particularly useful to them, they can carry it around. It can be programmed to send reminders and messages, perhaps a one hour 'warning' or 'reminder' before an upcoming event or meeting.

This way, they can make sure they are truly prepared, and handle their task or meet up with appointments with professional finesse.

Use Relaxation Techniques

If your partner is distracted or impulsive or has ADHD, this could become greater if they are under duress or stress. This is one of the strongest reasons why no matter how busy life seems to them, they should take breaks, and rest whether it is just working with imagery or meditation or deep breathing.

These things will enable them to remain focused and give them the time to reassess. Using a relaxation technique will give them the opportunity to recalibrate.

Take Notes

Taking them while they are in a meeting or speaking over the phone can help them to remember certain information accurately. The notetaking can help them to highlight new items in their A, B, and C lists. The benefits are simply multiple.

If they have issues processing some auditory information in a board meeting and/ or become distracted, then they will realize that taking note is necessary.

Maintain a Routine

Tell your partner that maintaining a routine will enable them to achieve greater result. Anything they can over-learn will be very, very effective. If they are losing things constantly, it could add untold pressures to their life. So, they should have a routine and keep to it daily.

Surround Themselves with Efficient, Organized People

This is why you should build a support base for your partner, be really there for them. If they are in business or working for a corporation, they should surround themselves with people that are well organized.

At this point in their lives, they need to connect, and network with the right people; people that will help them to achieve their visions. Thus, getting along with the right people will be absolutely invaluable.

High-Functioning Social Anxiety

This is a mental disorder that affects millions of Americans. Many people who suffer from severe high-functioning social disorder get involved with varied treatment methods and efforts to get properly healed or get better to the extent that they can now be classified as becoming high-functioning.

High-functioning people can make sustained efforts, pursue careers and form relationships to fulfill their potentials in different areas of life.

Yet, they may continue to experience severe symptoms of anxiety that are life-altering and unpleasant. This is why people with high-functioning social anxiety are required to seek for treatment.

Social anxiety is the second most diagnosed type of anxiety disorder. People who suffer from this experience overwhelming fear of rejections and feelings of nervousness during social interactions, and this makes them to try to avoid such occasions if possible.

Patients with full-blown social anxiety disorder can be hugely affected by their social phobia and/ or experiencing difficulties in different areas of their lives. But this doesn't happen to chronic social anxiety disorder patients.

Most people experience this fear and anxiety, but it will prevent them to form relationships, volunteer to opportunities, fulfill their job descriptions, make speeches, perform or speak in public. These people are classified as having high-functioning social anxiety, which is stressful and unpleasant, but it doesn't keep them from living their normal life.

Signs of High-Functioning Social Anxiety

Symptoms of social anxiety disorder reinforce the patient's inability to communicate and socialize.

Social anxiety produces behavioral, emotional, psychological and physical symptoms. People who suffer from this are at normally at minimized levels of intensity. Here are some of the physical symptoms of social anxiety:

- *Rapid heartbeat*

- *Sweating*

- *Blushing*

- *Dizziness, lightheadedness*

- *Nausea or stomach cramps*

- *Trembling*

- *Difficulty breathing*

- *Dry mouth*

- *Issues thinking of the right words to use during presentation.*

Patients of high-functioning social anxiety disorder are always familiar with any of these symptoms. Although, they are not highly noticeable or manifest as strongly or as frequently as they do in people with social phobia. These symptoms can be really unpleasant and exhausting.

People living with high-functioning social anxiety disorders usually don't look forward in joyful hope to social events that are likely going to provoke such reactions.

The emotional and psychological symptoms of social anxiety can manifest either before, during or after social encounters. They include, but not limited to:

- *Constant fear of doing or saying embarrassing things*

- *Intense fear of rejection*

- *Extreme discomfort around significant orders like bosses*

- *Indisposition to express one's thoughts honestly and openly*

- *Obsession over negative outcomes and worst-case scenarios*

- *Paranoia and defensive when asking questions or looking for answers.*

- *Intense fear that anxiety reactions will be noticed by others.*

- *Becoming nervous or assuming that others are quick to judge and hostile*

- *Second-guessing and self-criticism after social encounters and much more.*

Those who live with social anxiety disorder suffers from disabling and excessive self-consciousness, this can make social interactions to be difficult to endure.

People with high- functioning social anxiety disorder also experience some of these fears and thoughts, but they developed strategies that enables them to push through the fear, connect, network and engage meaningfully with others when and where necessary.

Social anxiety disorder has a great impact on emotions and behaviors. People living with this condition go extra miles to avoid unnecessary social encounters. When interactions become readily unavoidable, they will either escape as quickly as they can or speak as little as they can, regardless of the shame or how their avoidable behavior makes them to feel.

They are comfortable with speaking or chatting with people online than speaking or chatting in person. They welcome every opportunity that will enable them to perform certain tasks alone than doing it in company of others.

People living with this condition may also avoid reaching out to certain people if they think it could be non-essential. But, they don't let their social phobia discourage them from doing things they love.

Their avoidant behavior are more controllable and restrained, to the extent that they can apply for jobs, find romantic partners, make new friends, seek for help when and where necessary, and do so many things which people with severe social anxiety finds disturbing or problematic.

But, the level of human relationship they initiate is still lesser than more outgoing people. Also, they tend to be uncomfortable around casual acquaintances or strangers. But, those with high-functioning social anxiety don't let opportunities to slip from their hands. They welcome satisfying experiences, and their lives are richer and extremely rewarding than people living with social anxiety disorder.

Transiting from Acute Social Anxiety to High-Functioning

The signs of people living with high-functioning social anxiety are usually moderate or mild. They experience more life-altering and stressful lifestyle than those with normal shyness. But their social anxiety is not intimidating or powerful enough to obstruct their ability to achieve their goals or build relationships.

But this is different for people with high-functioning social anxiety disorder. Their social symptoms are usually persistent and strong during childhood, adolescence and even as young adults, thereby reducing their activities in multiple ways and inhibiting their capacity as they search for ultimate happiness and fulfillment. After some time they were able to handle their social anxiety, and finally learn to finally break out of their shell or self-imposed social exile.

People overcome their social anxiety symptoms for several reasons. Some people who recover from social anxiety disorder succeed after getting the needed treatment. Research says that with a combination of medication, and psychotherapy, some patients can learn how to manage their symptoms, and this may decline in intensity if treatment continues to happen for an extended period.

Although treatment for social anxiety disorder is very important, there are other helpful tips that can help patients' transit from severe to high-functioning social anxiety. Here are some of the factors:

Self- Help

There are many self-help books that explain strategies or techniques for overcoming their nervousness. In addition to treatment, many people living with social anxiety disorder can sign up for courses that will teach them communication methods or skills that will enable them to overcome self-esteem problems or shyness.

Social media and online forums also provide more options to help socially anxious people looking for moral support and advice. Online friends, taking classes and reading some self-help books could be helpful, but they are extremely insufficient to replace organized treatment. Taking the necessary treatment would be more impactful.

Mind-Body Healing Techniques

Over the years, people have benefitted hugely from holistic wellness practices as health-boosting effects of meditation, yoga, Tai Chi, massage therapy, art therapy, music, biofeedback, hypnosis, and a host of other mind-body techniques keep on spreading consistently.

Some residential mental treatment centers provide awesome healing practices as part of their recovery process. This shows how they work both in and outside rehabilitation.

Holistic mind-body practices are capable of helping social anxiety patients relieve stress and aids in ongoing re-training of the brain to react with less paranoia and fear during social interactions.

Reduction in Intensity Related to Aging

A study of social anxiety disorder observed that about 37% of patients within the last twelve years period experienced significant improvement even without receiving any treatment. This is lower than the recovery rate for panic disorders which was 82% and generalized anxiety disorder which was about 58%. So, treatment remains very essential for patients suffering from severe social anxiety issues.

Why It Is Necessary to Take Care of Life's Necessities

Irrespective of the complex nature of initial social phobia issues, some social anxiety patients must fulfill certain life goals and / or responsibilities in order to live happily or succeed.

This could mean satisfying all academic requirements, enrolling for a course or degree, fulfilling all workplace duties and assignments, interviewing for jobs, and much more. Many social disorder patients are reaching out to others for love or friendship, and that is easier to do through lots of online forums.

Treatment for High-Functioning and Social Anxiety Disorder

Those with high-functioning anxiety are better and more privileged than people living with social anxiety disorder. Usually, they earn their peak performance status through dedicated effort, hard work, and an ongoing commitment to treatment, this is an avenue for recovery.

Those who have been high functioning for some years are recommended to try inpatient treatment method, especially those of them that are suffering in silence despite their outward appearances.

With round-the-clock and intensive treatment services in a fully functional environment, patients with high-functioning social anxiety can get relief from their symptoms, which may remain limiting, stress-inducing and unpleasant in multiple ways regardless of not being fully debilitating.

For people living with mild-to-moderate social anxiety, inpatients and outpatients' treatments are highly recommended and usually highly effective for those that are experiencing it at any level of intensity.

Things You Shouldn't Say to an Anxious Partner

Today, you know your partner is suffering from anxiety disorder. Here are top things you shouldn't say to them:

Calm Down

It could be ineffective to tell your partner who is suffering from anxiety disorder to calm down. Doing so is like telling someone who is suffering from fever to stop sneezing. To be anxious means to be in a state of near-constant or constant stress or depression. You don't have to say this to them. In fact, telling them to calm down could be an unpleasant sensation, and counter-productive.

Even when you command them to calm down, many people could not. To some people, such words can add to their anxiety level, because they feel guilty or become frustrated due to their inability to calm down, which you have asked them to do.

It Is in Your Head

Really? This is 100% untrue. However, most people suffering from anxiety have been forced to hear these words from their respective partners a couple of times. Some of the symptoms occur when the brain begins to play tricks and/ or act hyper-aware.

But, when you tell them that it is all in their heads, it implies that what they are feeling is a make-believe horror story. This is false.

Anxiety is not a child's play, it is not amusing, not a playful make-believe. It is a hellish reality, omnipresent and highly terrifying experience which is presently affecting millions of people around the world.

It Is Not a Big Deal

Saying things like this is also counterproductive. By telling your partner it is not a big deal, you are simply invalidating their feelings and mental illness. Although, most anxious partners worry about trivial issues, sometimes their thoughts and actions are often irrational, but it is difficult to control how these things affect you.

This is exactly how anxiety works. You don't have to confirm that the things they pass through is not a big deal, by confirming this you are indirectly saying that the sufferings they endure due to their anxious state is also not a big deal.

I Know How You Feel

I bet you, although many people say this, but I guarantee you that obviously you have no idea how they feel. Unless you have previously experienced anxiety. It will be difficult for you to possibly understand how anxiety works, and what your partner is truly passing through.

Imagine a non-diabetic patient telling a diabetic patient that they know what they are passing through. You may have a rough idea of what it could mean if you were told, by someone who has experienced it previously.

But, you don't know truly how the person is feeling or feels. It is insulting to tell your partner you know how they are feeling, when in essence you have no idea of their condition.

Have a Cup of Drink, You Will Feel Better

This is a standard tradition in most cultures to provide your partner with a cup of alcoholic beverage when they feel angry, upset, tired or sad or experiencing certain negative emotions. Admittedly, sometimes it works in the short-term. However, anxiety is not a short-term issue, it is unrelenting and constant.

So, trying to calm someone's anxiety level with a cup of drink will work on a temporary basis, it is not a permanent cure. It can only work for some hours before the hangover will be gone, and they will be back to sober mood as well as feeling anxious again.

Anxiety can effectively be treated with healthier, better, and long-lasting ways. Thus, trying to solve the complication with alcohol will invite the risk of dependency and/ or addiction.

Stop Complaining

Telling your partner to shut up and stop complaining that other people are suffering from same condition is counterproductive. Anxious people feel of sensations such as panic, fear, worry and lots more. One of the strongest emotions they feel that doesn't attract much attention is the feeling of guilt.

Your partner may be feeling guilt for what may happen to them in future, what they are unclear whether it will happen or not. There are many out there who is going through this now, and to say these to them is just to add to the guilt they are already feeling.

Why Can't You Tell Me What Is Wrong with You?

Many patients of anxiety find it difficult to communicate their true feelings or what is wrong with them. Some of them may even feel embarrassed or ashamed to be anxious. Some may lack the appropriate words to explain their anxiety properly.

Your partner may even not be disposed to you how they feel, for whatever reason. I can understand when you are trying to help a loved one, and it turns out that the person doesn't want to tell you what is wrong. But, trying to make them to feel guilty about their silence won't solve the problem.

So, the antidote is to let them know that you care and cherish them, you are there for them. However, if you have issues in reaching out to you or in communicating to you their real feelings, please don't take it for granted. Don't give up in showing them love, and they may be inspired to reach out.

You Should Try Veganism/ Yoga / Meditation

This is not in contrast to what I have said earlier. The health benefits of veganism, yoga, meditation and others are multiple. They have been found out to be extremely helpful to people dealing with anxiety. For example, I have recommended meditation strongly in this book. Yes, it has been observed to work wonders for some people.

However, it is important you also know that it doesn't work for everybody. So, if you push your partner towards a particular activity, only for them to discover that it doesn't help their situation, it could exceedingly be frustrating. Find out if meditation or any of these recommended activities work for them.

You will be able to know this when they have tried it for a while. So, to be on the right tract, you can suggest varied anxiety-curbing activities for them, but don't make the mistake of pressuring them to accept anything they don't want to do.

Surprising Health Benefits of Hugging

Brain scientists have shown that hugging or a loving touch to your loved one who is currently living with anxiety disorder could be therapeutic. It can:

- *Support their immune system*

- *Lower their blood pressure*

- *Lower their heart rate*

- *Lower their cortisol levels*

- *Improve sleep*

- *Stimulate their brain's memory centers*

- *Prompt positive emotions*

- *Make them feel happier, better and healthier.*

- *Reduce anxiety*

- *Reduce pain*

The importance of hugs and simple touch can never be overemphasized. Stories abound of premature babies, adults and children, pregnant women, elderly populations and spouses with emotional problems or chronic pain conditions whose health have improved due to interventions of massage, hugs, or touch.

To most people, hugging is a natural phenomenon; they do it as frequent as possible. South Americans, Italians and French touch more frequently than most people in other parts of the world.

Your partner needs frequent hugs or non-sexual touch like they need oxygen. When you do this genuinely, it will inspire them to be more open to giving and receiving it too. The way you touch your partner speaks volumes.

Types of Hugs and Their Meanings

A hug can convey lots of meaning to your loved one. The message you are sending while hugging is paramount, and you should be aware of it. Here are types of hugs and their meanings.

Bear Hug

This type of hug worth a million words; it is reassuring, passionate and tight. This is the type of hug shared by people that love and cherish each other. It's the type of hug you have been getting from your siblings and parents- a warm embrace that relieves you of anxiety and stress.

If you share this type of hug to your loved one, it means you have deep feelings of emotions for them.

Polite Hug

This is the type of hug that exists between colleagues, peers and acquaintances. It is usually given sideways oftentimes with hands around the waist, with just a partial-upper body contact. In a polite hug, the lower body doesn't connect with each other, indicating some awkwardness or discomfort. If you are giving your loved one, this type of hug, it means there is some distance in the relationship. Avoid polite hug.

One -Way Hug

This is an embarrassing type of hug. You are genuinely hugging someone with everything you got, yet the receiver is adamant; couldn't even lift an arm around your shoulder. This is called giving a one-way hug. The noticeable lack of reciprocation from the other person shows that they don't love and care for you as you would, and they don't love you as you truly deserve.

Intimate hug

This is an intimate, full-body and close-embrace with eye contact. The eye contact makes the hug more amazing and takes it to a whole new level. It is clearly and absolutely more than a physical touch. Intimate hug tends to connect the hearts together, beating for each other. If you are receiving or giving this type of hug, it is an indication that both of you share something in common.

Buddy Hug

This is another type of sideway hug, where your arms are on each other's waist or shoulders. It is a level of trust and comfort that transcends your daily romance. Giving your loved one a buddy hug exemplifies clear intimacy and love.

It means that both of you aren't couples, but just friends. Sharing this type of hug while you are walking or sitting shows that your relationship is meant to last in perpetuity.

Back Hug

This is also another type of intimate hug. Giving or receiving a back hug is a sign of trust and protection. This is the form of hugs kids give their parents, which parents willingly reciprocate by carrying and playing with them.

If you are giving your loved one this type of hug, it literally means that you got their back, you are ever willing to protect them whether in good or bad times, and you will always be there for them.

Each hug of these hugs should last for at least 20 seconds so that you can release oxytocin, a hormone that lowers anxiety and relaxes your loved one. Continuous hugging is therapeutic. Oxytocin is a beautiful hormone in the body which scientists refer as the 'cuddle hormone'. Levels of cuddle hormone rise when sit close, touch or hug each other. It reduces blood pressure too.

EVALUATION AND CONCLUSION

Anxiety is an awkward situation. It ranges from an intensely uncomfortable situation to a vague apprehension similar to fear or stress. It is a normal part of being human. It is a warning signal, often triggered by either a conscious or unconscious perception of danger. It can be experienced physically, mentally, and psychologically.

Some of the physical symptoms include:

- *Pounding heart*

- *Trembling or muscle tension*

- *Light-headedness or dizziness*

- *Flushed, feeling hot or sweating*

- *Breathing difficulties, tightness in throat or chest.*

- *Waking too early, or in the night or trouble falling asleep.*

- *Indigestion, nausea, low appetite.*

Mental symptoms include:

- *Sweating*

- *Feeling nervous*

- *Feeling tired or weak and lots more*

Cognitive and psychological symptoms include:

- *Paranoia, trust issues*

- *Self-doubt, self-criticism*

- *Specific fears like fear of crowds, fear of heights*

- *Thinking or feeling something will go wrong or something is wrong*

- *Distractibility, lack of focus or poor concentration*

These are natural symptoms, and from time to time, people experience them. But, it gets to a point when anxiety will become severe or extreme to the extent that it will interfere with your partner's day to day activity. In this case, one will need to consider whether the disorder will require some type of treatment or not.

Anxiety disorder is a serious mental issue in the United States, which is affecting about 18% of people each year. However, due to the fact that anxiety is normal for most people, it won't be easy to determine when it has become a problem. Two most critical questions to consider include:

- *Is anxiety part of an ongoing or repeated pattern?*

- *How much does your partner experience it?*

If a repeated pattern increases to the level where it interferes with your partners ability to work, where it is hard to control, or to build quality relationships, your partner could be said to be affected by anxiety disorder.

The natural warning signs are complex- anxiety can show up in multiple ways. It is a rare occurrence that could be triggered by a host of specific situations. It is subtly distracting us, always present and wearing us down. Some of the common issues are described below:

Generalized Anxiety Disorder

This involves anxiety of varied areas or day to day worry such as self-image, money, health, day-to-day tasks, relationships, school or wok. This condition as the name implies is simply generalized, it is not focused on one specific thing.

This is an issue that develops gradually. It can begin at any point in life, but gradually develops between childhood and adulthood. Generalized anxiety disorder can be accompanied by substance abuse, and depression. It can be mild, severe, and moderate and the level of its severity will depend on how the patient can function.

Phobias

This anxiety disorder involves fear of specific situation or thing such as spiders, enclosed spaces, crowds etc. It is a discomfort or fear triggered by situations or occasions that interferes with social life, school or other important areas of living. Phobias are very common and affects about 4-5% of U.S population annually and about 11% of people in their lifetime.

Panic Disorder

This type of anxiety includes repeated episodes of panic, which can come unexpectedly. Symptoms include:

- *Chest pain or racing heart*

- *Choking feeling or shortness of breath*

- *Hot flashes, chills or sweating*

- *Shaking, dizziness or nausea*

- *Going crazy or fear of dying.*

In some people, some of these attacks come out of the blues, while in others they are triggered by specific circumstances. Some people develop panic disorder by experiencing panic attack. Intense anxiety regarding a panic attack can lead to avoidance of not going out or crowds, which can result in social isolation.

Obsessive-Compulsive Disorder

Obsessive-compulsive disorder includes compulsions or obsessions that interfere with life. Obsessions refers to intrusive images or thoughts that recur in the mind despite series of attempts to halt them such as fears that something may happen to your work, home, or to a loved one or excessive worries about germs.

Compulsion are behaviors that decrease or an attempt to prevent anxiety. It interferes with our daily activities. It is hard to control. Compulsion takes up excessive time such as hand-washing or excessive cleaning and needing to check and cross check things multiple times. Obsessive-compulsive disorder affects about 2 to 3% of the U.S population.

Post-Traumatic Stress Disorder

This includes a reaction to witnessing or experiencing a frightening event like having a serious accident, being raped or assaulted and much more. Those who suffer from post-traumatic stress disorder:

- *Re-examine or re-experience the event through waking 'flashbacks' or nightmares.*

- *Avoid situations or places that reminds them of the event*

- *Feel emotionally numb or have partial amnesia as a way of relieving the experience psychologically.*

- *Experiences symptoms of arousal such as being easily startled or flabbergasted.*

- *Often have poor concentration or insomnia.*

Triggers or Causes of Anxiety

Anxiety is often triggered by a combination of environmental and genetic factors. It can be as a result of certain underlying medical conditions such as:

- *A drug*

- *Thyroid disorder*

- *Cocaine*

- *Amphetamines*

- *Ecstasy and other substances*

The presence of anxiety disorder can result to substance abuse, as way to try to self-medicate or treat it. Always remember that anxiety can coexist with other forms of depressions and disorders.

Treatment

Anxiety disorder can be combated with a wide range of effective treatments. Treatments can come in two categories namely:

- *Psychotherapy*

- *Pharmacotherapy*

Psychotherapy

This involves the use of a licensed therapist. This could be a psychologist, psychiatrist, licensed family or marriage counselor, and licensed clinical social worker. Behavioral therapy remains the most commonly treatment method of anxiety disorders.

Psychotherapy involves series of controlled exposure to the things that causes or triggers anxiety plus coping skills, and it equips the person living with anxiety disorder how to deal with it. Consulting with a therapist can help to navigate this process.

A therapist can also recommend other helpful tips like websites, apps, and self-help books along with the therapy. The benefits of treatment are multiple such as:

- *Greater insights*

- *Reduced symptoms*

- *Improved coping skills*

- *Feeling supported and understood*

- *Better overall quality of life and lots more.*

The only drawbacks to therapy are the cost, effort and time involved.

Pharmacotherapy

This is the art of using psychotropic medications prescribed by a physician or a psychiatrist. Two essential medications that are commonly used to treat anxiety are:

- *Antidepressants*

- *Benzodiazepines*

Antidepressants are helpful in treating the ailment for long-term, and it takes a few weeks before you can start seeing the effective results. While, benzodiazepines provide short-term relief. Continuous use of it can lead to depression and dependence.

Also, other non-benzodiazepine and non-antidepressants medications are also used to treat anxiety disorders.

Discontinuation of medications can make the patient to be vulnerable to a risk of relapse. There are some times when your partner's anxiety reaction will become so intense, to the extent that therapy alone will be ineffective in resolving the mental condition. If this happens, a therapist will use a combination of medications to make it happen.

Helping Yourself

Yes, your partner is the victim, you are the one helping them to get relieved, and live better. You are the one tolerating them. So, you really need to help yourself. Here are some of the things that have worked for others over the years, I am passionately optimistic that they will work for you if you try:

- Calm yourself down with proven techniques such as relaxation, mindfulness and slow breathing.

- Think carefully about your partner's worries. Let them know that you are optimistic they will be fine someday.

- You can distract your partner by helping them do something they enjoy. This could be having an in-depth conversation with them, taking lunch together during workplace break, reading a book, going for a walk, taking time to play with a pet, doing some gardening etc.

- Brainstorm and come up some solutions. Put your best to ensure that your partner enjoys serenity of mind and body.

- Take one step at a time, no matter how small, and gradually you will win the race.

Managing Your Partner's Anxiety in the Long Term

- You really need to learn the appropriate way to confront all the things you are anxious about. Begin with the less scary, and gradually transit to the ones you worry most about.

- Learn about anxiety, how it works, what triggers, and how to deal with it, especially when it has affected a loved one.

- Join a support group, either online or offline.

- Encourage your partner to get involved with at least 30 minutes of physical exercises daily. The benefits of exercises can never be overemphasizing; it helps in reducing your anxiety level and changes your brain.

- Encourage them to spend quality time with friends and family, those whose company they admire, especially those who can manage their stress level.

- Tell your partner to be aware of depression, because many people living with anxiety disorders are also affected by depression.

- Talk to their therapists if they are having trouble cutting down on their drugs, or alcohol intake.

- Caffeine and smoking can worsen their situations. If they smoke, encourage them to quit, and try as much as possible to cut down on their intake of cola, tea, coffee, food and drinks that contains volume of caffeine.

- Support their decisions to seek treatment.

- Ask them if they would like to talk, and be there for them. Listen to their concerns with sympathy. Giving them a listening ear will work wonders. It will motivate them to talk even when they are not ready to talk. Knowing that someone is there for them can be helpful.

- Be sensitive to their feelings when you are offering them advice. The same thing applies when you are trying to explain to them to reduce their fears, worries or anxieties.

- It could be counter-productive to tell an anxiety patient to snap out of it or relax.

How to Deal with Anxiety in a Relationship

Anxiety is a treatable issue; but this happens only when those suffering from it can seek help. One of your prime jobs is to graciously and gently ask them to seek for support. You can remind them this is a mental illness and tell them how important it is for them to seek for a professional assistance.

No matter the situation, you should offer them undying love, affection and care. They should know you are there for them, regardless of the situation. There are many certified mental health professionals around who are trained and overtly available to help your loved one struggling with anxiety disorder right now.

Understanding, helping, coping and loving someone with anxiety comes with a plethora of challenges. At the end of the day, it is not just about you, it is about their recovery process. When a loved one is suffering from anxiety, nothing would be more life-affirming, comforting and appealing than knowing that there is someone out there who is by their side, and who is ever willing to help them navigate the situation. This is where you should come in.

If you decide to love someone with anxiety, you may experience days where you will feel you have done so much already like taking a thousand steps. It may come to a time when you may be at the verge of giving up. That is normal. That is understandable.

However, if you can take time to go through the crucibles of loving your loved one who is living with anxiety together, this will lighten and spice your relationship, and make your relationship to grow richer, deeper, stronger, and makes it worth it at the end.

You are currently in a relationship with someone you love. You have learned their communication styles, established boundaries, and developed trust.

Constantly, you may be questioning your relationship, yourself and even your partner. You may be asking yourself series of questions, like with this relationship last? How do you know if you are living with the right person, what if you are not capable of maintaining a committed, healthy relationship?

This consistent worrying is known as 'relationship anxiety'. It refers to doubt, insecurity and feelings of worry that can pop up in a relationship if everything is not going as earlier planned.

Is Relationship Anxiety Normal?

Astrid Robertson, an erudite psychologist that helps patients with relationship issues has confirmed that this is normal. Many people experience relationship anxiety at the beginning of their union, even before they know their partners too well or when they are unsure they need the relationship.

These feelings can also exist in long-term, committed relationships. Studies have proven that overtime relationship anxiety can give rise to:

- *Stomach upset*

- *Lack of motivation*

- *Emotional exhaustion or fatigue*

- *Emotional stress and other physical concerns.*

Your partner's anxiety can lead to behaviors that will create untold distress and issues to you and your partner.

Signs of Relationship Anxiety

This can come up in different ways. At some point, some people will feel insecure about their relationships, especially in the early stage, when they are at the verge of dating and forming a commitment.

This is not unusual. These anxious thoughts can grow creeper and deeper into your everyday life. Below are some potential signs:

Wondering If Your Partner Love You In The First Place

Astrid Robertson explains that when relationship anxiety strikes, one of the commonest questions you will be asking yourself repeatedly is whether you matter to your partner in the first. This poses a huge question to the fundamental need to feel secure, belong, and connect in a partnership.

For example, you may be concerned that:

- *Your partner may never miss you if you travel for a long time.*

- *They only want to be with you because of what they will gain from you.*

- *Should anything unexpected happen to you, they may be ineligible to offer help or support.*

Doubting If They Have Feelings for You

You may have exchanged marital vows with your loved. You may be happy to be around them, bringing them lunch, taking a walk with them or playing with them. Yet, they seem to be unconcerned about you.

You may be wondering whether they love you in the first. Maybe they love you, but are slow to show it or respond to noticeable physical affection. Maybe they are not willing to reply to text for a few hours, even days.

When you are a little distant from them, you may be wondering if they have affectionate feelings towards you.

Keep in mind that many people have this feeling from time to time, and these worries or anxieties can become more intense if your partner has relationship anxiety.

You May Be Wondering Whether They Want a Break

A good relationship can make you and your partner feel happy, secure, and loved. It is good to hold tenaciously to these feelings and hoping that nothing truncates or disrupt the relationship.

Occupying yourself with these thoughts can get to the point of making your partner to leave you. To secure their continued affection, you are advised to adjust some of your behavior, and develop tolerance in your relationship.

Doubting Whether You Are Compatible

Relationship anxiety is enough to make you to doubt whether you are truly compatible with your partner, even things are going as expected in the relationship. You may occupy your minds with different thoughts such as wondering if you are truly happy or whether you just think you are.

You may be focusing your attention on slight differences- your partner loves reading to poems, but you are more a self-help book reader.

Sabotaging Your Relationship

There are multiple ways your loved one can sabotage your relationship such as:

- *Repeatedly picking quarrels with you*

- *Pushing the thoughts away when you are held down by distress.*

- *Testing their relationship boundaries by taking a walk or going for lunch with their ex without telling you.*

Guaranteed, that some partners may even do these things intentionally, but the underlying effect is whether to realize whether they love you, and how much they love and care for you.

Causes of Relationship Anxiety

Identifying the cause of relationship anxiety can take time focused self-exploration. Because it doesn't have a single cause. You may have issues trying to identify the potential causes of this mental condition.

You may not even be aware what causes it, but no matter how it presents itself, the underlying reason reflects a deep yearning for connection. There are some common factors that may have played a key role here such as:

- *You or your partner's previous relationship experiences*

- *Low self-esteem*

- *Attachment styles, and*

- *A tendency to question*

You or Your Partner's Previous Relationship Experiences

Remembering what has happened in the past, can affect you or your partner, even when you think you have gotten over them. Relationship anxiety may likely exist in your relationship if in the past, your partner:

- *Cheated on you or you cheated on them*

- *Dumped you for someone else*

- *Misled you into thinking they love you*

- *Lied about their true feelings towards you and much more.*

If you have been deeply hurt in the past, you may have issues loving your partner again. Certain triggers whether you are aware of it or not can provoke insecurity, doubt and remind you of the past.

Low Self-Esteem

Low self-esteem can lead to relationship anxiety and insecurity. An old research suggests that people with low self-esteem are most likely going to doubt their partner's feelings when they are experiencing doubts.

Also, feeling disappointed about yourself is enough to make you think that your partner feels the same way towards you.

Attachment Style

The attachment style you have in your childhood can influence your relationship. If your caregiver or parent respond to your needs effectively, offered the needed help and support, you may probably develop a secure attachment style.

But, if they didn't and allowed you to develop independently, your level of attachment style will be less secure. Insecure attachment can lead to relationship anxiety complications in multiple ways.

CONCLUSION

No relationship is immune from having issues. It is not easy to avoid relationship anxiety. But there are certain things you can do to enjoy life with your partner and deal with anxiety disorder effectively.

Supporting your partner with anxiety can be truly challenging. To navigate this process, patience and understanding are needed. It is your responsibility to make your partner to be remain calm, and resolute even in the face of disturbing scenarios.

Your relationship can suffer, your communication can erode, and your barriers can rear up. People living with generalized anxiety disorder for example are twice more likely going to experience relationship issues like arguing and the risk of avoiding intimacy says Anxiety and Depression Association of America (ADAA).

Difficulties can spill over your professional life, your finances and the way you socialize with your loved one. This can make your partner to start feeling depressed or anxious. Yes, there are multiple ways of treating anxiety, but becoming a highly supportive partner can be extremely helpful.

Anxiety attack is very terrifying, but it can't kill. However, when the patient is experiencing a full-blown anxiety attack, the symptoms- difficulty breathing, racing heart, flushing skin, and chest pain can make the person feel they will faint, die or lose their minds.

Anxiety doesn't really go with age; it doesn't vanish. It can be compared with other forms of feelings like love, anger, frustration, happiness, sadness and so on. Just like it is difficult to eliminate those sensations from your brain, it will be difficult for you to get rid of anxiety from your brain.

Can anxiety be treated medically? You can win the battle without applying any medication. Sometimes all you need to overcome nervousness and worry is to modify your lifestyle, thoughts and behavior. First, a drug-free may be ideal, then if the symptoms persists, worsen or don't improve, then you can speak with a doctor.

Anxiety is a chronic condition that can take different forms, depending on the severity of the condition. Most people with panic disorder and phobias improve greatly within a few days or first weeks of proper treatment.

Can your loved one recover fully from anxiety disorder? Yes, they can, if they get the required support and treatment.

Can anxiety affect your marriage? Oftentimes when anxiety strikes, it breaks down connection and trust. It causes worry or fear. It can make you feel less of the real needs of your partner or if you feel overwhelmed by your partner's present condition.

Hugging your partner is one of the surprising health benefits of anxiety attacks. It does so much than making the person feel good for a moment. Further research says that hugging lowers the risk of anxiety and help to reduce stress, different forms of illnesses and depression. A simple hug is therapeutic to anxiety patients.

When your partner is affected by anxiety, be with them, and reassure them of your undying love and affection. This could help them to move towards getting realistic solutions. Love your partner today, and you will be happy you did.

Thank you for downloading this book! I hope it helped you to understand, help, cope and live with someone with anxiety. The next step is to practice all you have learnt.

Lastly, if you enjoyed this book, then, I'd like to ask you for a favor, would you be kind enough to leave a review for this book on Amazon? It'd be greatly appreciated!

Thank you again and good luck!

www.ingramcontent.com/pod-product-compliance
Lightning Source LLC
Chambersburg PA
CBHW051955150726
47999CB00004B/1387